CIVIC PARTICIPATION IN AMERICA

CIVIC PARTICIPATION IN AMERICA

Quentin Kidd

First published in hardcover in 2011 by PALGRAVE MACMILLAN® in the United States—a division of St. Martin's Press LLC, 175 Fifth Avenue, New York, NY 10010.

Where this book is distributed in the UK, Europe and the rest of the world, this is by Palgrave Macmillan, a division of Macmillan Publishers Limited, registered in England, company number 785998, of Houndmills, Basingstoke, Hampshire RG21 6XS.

Palgrave Macmillan is the global academic imprint of the above companies and has companies and representatives throughout the world.

Palgrave® and Macmillan® are registered trademarks in the United States, the United Kingdom, Europe and other countries.

ISBN: 978–1–137–37177–5

The Library of Congress has cataloged the hardcover edition as follows:

Kidd, Quentin.
    Civic participation in America / Quentin Kidd.
        p. cm.
    Includes bibliographical references.
    ISBN 978–0–230–11134–9
        1. Political participation—United States. 2. Citizenship—United States. 3. Civics. I. Title.

JK1764.K53 2011
323'.0420973—dc23   2011017515

A catalogue record of the book is available from the British Library.

Design by MPS Limited, A Macmillan Company

First PALGRAVE MACMILLAN paperback edition: December 2013

10 9 8 7 6 5 4 3 2 1

Contents

Figures, Photos, and Tables

Figures

Photos

Tables

Acknowledgments

This book has its roots in an invitation from a colleague and nationally recognized civic entrepreneur, Greg Werkheiser. In the summer of 1999, Greg invited me to help him and another colleague, Martin Haley, launch a new youth civic engagement program. My role was to design and teach one part of the curriculum. The goal of the program, which is now part of the Sorensen Institute for Political Leadership at the University of Virginia, was to provide young Virginians with the knowledge and skills necessary to be effective leaders and advocates at the state and local levels. Over the course of ten years of teaching in this program and interacting with the students, I came to appreciate the role of history and institutions on our civic participation. In conducting a search of the literature to learn more about it, I discovered a dearth of scholarship and this book is an attempt to fill that void by just a little bit. It is dedicated to the hundreds and hundreds of students with whom I have had the pleasure to teach and discuss these ideas over the years.

I am fortunate to be at a wonderful place at which to teach and do scholarship. Christopher Newport University has provided encouragement and all of the support I have needed to do this work, including providing me with several small grants, a sabbatical leave, and time in the summers at Harris Manchester College, University of Oxford, to write and reflect. I have also been fortunate at CNU to have the support and encouragement of Harry and Judy Wason. Additionally, I am continuously appreciative of Irwin Morris at the University of Maryland, College Park, for being an excellent academic role model and for helpful encouragement and timely advice. Finally, I am eternally grateful for the wonderful support, patience, and encouragement of my wife, Holly.

CHAPTER 1

INTRODUCTION: THE CALCULUS
FOR CIVIC PARTICIPATION

Photo 1.1 Portrait of Thomas Jefferson

Thomas Jefferson was among the most prominent colonial-era leaders who believed that civic and political participation should be motivated by a sense of duty.

Source: Prints & Photographs Division, Library of Congress, LC-USZ62-53985

Photo 1.2   Portrait of James Madison
James Madison argued that people were inherently motivated to participate in civic and political life by selfish motives.
Source: Prints & Photographs Division, Library of Congress, LC-USZ62-87924

The day after the 2008 presidential election, I asked my students who had voted to write down on an index card their top reason for voting; if they had not, I asked for the top reason they did not vote. Of those who voted, nearly eight in ten gave a response that I would consider self-interested: based upon some selfish or self-serving objective ranging from strong support or opposition to a policy to fear of being ridiculed by friends if they did not vote. The remaining students gave responses that I would consider civically oriented: voting because they felt a duty or obligation to do so.[1] Here are a few explanations I received from those students who said they voted.

> I voted. The war . . . . We need to get out of Iraq. It's a mistake and I just don't want to see more people killed for a

mistake. It's hurting everything, the economy, our relations with other countries, the price of gas, everything. Totally the war . . .

Yes. I voted for John McCain. I support the War on Terrorism and John McCain does too.

I voted because as a black woman I am inspired by Barack Obama. I also strongly support health care for everyone and Obama supports that. My grandmother had to sell her house and move in with my family because her health care expenses were too much.

I've voted ever since I was old enough. When I was a kid I went with my parents to vote. It's just habit now. It's the right thing to do. I voted for Obama.

A few days after the election, I was sitting in my favorite coffee shop grading papers and a small group of thirty-something women walked in and sat down at a table near me. I knew one of them casually and we exchanged waves. It soon became apparent that this was a local elementary school's Parent Teacher's Association (PTA) meeting. On my way out, I stopped to say hello to my casual acquaintance, and in the course of the conversation asked the group how long they had been involved in the PTA. The answers were not surprising: they had all been involved for as long as their own children had been enrolled in the school. One parent even admitted that she had joined a year before her child had started school so that she would already know the principal, teachers, and other PTA parents by the time her child arrived the next year.

Voting and serving on the PTA are acts of civic participation, and like all such acts, an individual must be motivated to engage in them. One could be motivated by some selfish interest or by a sense of civic obligation. There are many forces that might act upon a person to stimulate one or both of these motivations, and in this book I focus upon several societal-level forces—large-scale institutions within society—and ask whether the long- and short-term evolution of these institutions has altered the calculus for individual civic participation in America in such a way as to fundamentally favor the self-interest motivation over the civic duty motivation.

THE MOTIVATION FOR PARTICIPATION

Those students who said they voted expressed, to varying degrees, motivations for their actions that the framers of the constitution would likely be able to recognize. The founders saw two kinds of motivations for individual civic participation, and as expressed by my students and those PTA parents, the two kinds of motivations are still active today: self-interest (or liberal individualism) and civic duty (or republican communitarianism). We might think of these two motivations, as suggested by Campbell, as two ends of a spectrum (2006). Both philosophies had powerful advocates in the late-eighteenth century. Marone argues that the liberal philosophy is dominant, but that it has been continuously challenged during the course of American history by the republican philosophy (1990). While this cyclical view is appealing, I argue in this book that key social, economic, and political institutions have evolved over time in such a way as to strengthen the self-interest motivation and weaken the civic duty motivation for participation in more fundamental ways.

Among those who most clearly articulated the self-interest motivation for participation was James Madison. Weary of human nature, writing in *Federalist Ten* Madison argued that people were inherently motivated by selfish interests, and because of this government had to be structured to render the selfish motivations of groups of people (he called them factions) harmless to the political system. Madison argued that selfish motives were inherent: "The latent causes of faction are thus sown in the nature of man . . . A zeal for different opinions concerning religion, concerning government, and many other points, as well of speculation as of practice; an attachment to different leaders, . . . [s]o strong is this propensity of mankind, to fall into mutual animosities, that where no substantial occasion presents itself, the most frivolous and fanciful distinctions have been sufficient to kindle their unfriendly passions, and excite their most violent conflict" (1999 [1787], 47).

From the Madisonian perspective, then, politics is about conflict, and that conflict is at its heart over differing interests. Individuals participate in politics, Madison argued, to protect and advance serious concerns about their views on religion, the role of government, attachment to particular leaders, but they also participate in politics to protect and advance frivolous and fanciful concerns, and even the most minor differences can lead to enormous conflicts. The big question for Madison was not how to tamp down on these passions, but how to mediate them in such a way as to avoid a level of conflict that would destroy the political system.

Madison's view of politics as conflict is well represented in scholarship and practice, and by my students. Lasswell advanced what is perhaps the most commonly cited definition of politics as "who gets what, when, and how" (1950 [1932]), a definition that is about conflict over limited resources. Schattschneider's exploration of the "pressure system" in American politics is premised upon the idea that politics is, at its root, about private conflicts that have come to involve the wider public (1960). Both advocates of campaign finance reform and defenders of the current system of financing elections sound downright Madisonian in their recognition of the self-interest motivation and in their advocacy of reform or defense of the status quo. Supporters of reform argue that the political system is unfairly dominated by special interests that have an undue influence in the clashing of ideas in Washington. Defenders argue that placing limits on special interests will effectively limit their ability to fully engage in the conflict of ideas in Washington. Either way, the shadow of Madison looms large here.

Thomas Jefferson and George Washington stand out in their views that civic and political participation were motivated by a sense of duty to country and fellow man. Jefferson

was perhaps most idealistic in his belief that civic responsibility would overcome differing interests, telling Jean
Baptiste Say, "So invariably do the laws of nature create
our duties and interests, that when they seem to be at vari-
ance, we ought to suspect some fallacy in our reasonings."[2]
Washington, in a circular to the states in 1883, just before
resigning his commission and returning to private life, outlined four things that in his view were essential to the continued existence of the United States. Among these was a
sense of civic responsibility on the part of the people. "The
prevalence of that pacific and friendly disposition, among
the people of the United States, which will induce them
to forget their local prejudices and policies, to make those
mutual concessions which are requisite to the general prosperity, and in some instances, to sacrifice their individual
advantages to the interest of the community" (Allen 1988).
In his first inaugural address in 1789, Washington describes
his willingness to return to public life in terms of duty and
love for country. "I was summoned by my country, whose
voice I can never hear but with veneration and love . . ."
(*Inaugural Addresses 1989*).

Few have given descriptive power to this notion of participation driven by a sense of civic responsibility in America
as Alexis de Tocqueville did in *Democracy in America*. Tocqueville was writing in the 1830s just as Jacksonian politics
began to shift political power away from the founding elite
to the common man. Tocqueville admired the "skill with
which the inhabitants of the United States succeed in pro-
posing a common object to the exertions of a great many
men, and in inducing them voluntarily to pursue it . . .
As soon as [people] have taken up an opinion or a feeling
which they wish to promote in the world, they look out
for mutual assistance; and as soon as they have found each
other out, they combine" (1956 [1832]).

The civic duty view of participation is also well represented in scholarship, practice, and to a lesser extent by my
students. In his study of why people get involved in politics,
for example, Lane notes that in American political culture

a citizen's duty is defined in part as a duty to participate in community life and that this duty is toward the nation's forbears, family and children, posterity, and to others who take the time and effort to participate (1959). Campbell et al. (1954) and Campbell et al. (1960) demonstrate empirically that many citizens vote out of a sense of civic duty. Campbell has recently concluded the same thing, noting "an internalized sense of civic duty is an important factor in motivating people to cast a ballot" (2006, 180).

Presidents often rhetorically call Americans to service, but John F. Kennedy's 1961 inaugural address stands out in this regard. In reciting the troubles that face the nation, Kennedy tells Americans that the final success or failure of the country rests in their hands, that the "trumpet summons us again . . . to bear the burden of a long twilight struggle . . . a struggle against the common enemies of man: tyranny, poverty, disease, and war itself." He then draws the speech to a close with the famous line: "And so, my fellow Americans: ask not what your country can do for you—ask what you can do for your country" *(Inaugural Addresses 1989)*.

While not as well represented as it once was (as we will see later in Chapter 5), the sentiment toward citizen responsibilities and duties is represented in high school civics education across the country. For example, one well-used civics textbook tells students, "The system of democratic government that we support emphasizes the importance of 'rule by the people.' One aspect of 'ruling' is citizen participation" (Wolfson 2005). Another high school civics workbook includes a section on the Rights and Responsibilities of Citizens, and sounds Tocquevillian in its description: " . . . for society to be successful, citizens must also assume duties and responsibilities. Students will discuss some of these rights and responsibilities. They will work together to make decisions . . ." *(Civic Participation Activities Guide no date)*.

It is clear, then, that the two motivations for citizen participation seen by the American founders still resonate powerfully today. For Marone the story of America is the story of a recurring political cycle, where these two motivations jostle with one another for preeminence. At certain points in the cycle, the republican impulse responds to political stalemate caused by privileged political interests protecting their gains with calls for reform and popular participation. Once the reform has taken place and the dust has settled, new privileged political interests become established, and the cycle starts anew. *The Democratic Wish*, as Marone calls it, is for popular participation, but the equilibrium that results from the cycle is a liberal one (1990, 9–14).

From this perspective, citizen participation in civic and political life would be highest during periods of republican reform and lowest during periods of liberal equilibrium, where protection of interests dominates. Yet, it is not unreasonable to ask whether the very cycle that Marone describes, a cycle of reform and retrenchment, is associated with fundamental changes in key institutions within society over time in such a way that the calculus for participation is also fundamentally changed. Critical junctures and long-term processes in American political development have affected important macro-institutions in such a way as to fundamentally alter the motivation for participation.

We can see the changed calculus reflected in national surveys. For instance, a 2006 Civic and Political Health of the Nation survey funded by The Pew Charitable Trusts found Americans largely motivated by self-interest when it comes to civic and political participation. The nationally representative sample of 2,232 people aged 15 and older found a slight majority of respondents saying it was their choice to get involved rather than their responsibility to get involved. Respondents were asked which statement they agreed with more: "It is my RESPONSIBILITY to get involved to make things better for society" or "It is my CHOICE to get involved to make things better for society." A clear majority of 53 percent said CHOICE, while only 40 percent said RESPONSIBILITY.

Similar views were reflected in respondents' reporting why they voted in elections. More respondents (34 percent)

Table 1.1   Motivations for participation among Americans

"Which statement do you agree with more?"

40.3%—It is my RESPONSIBILITY to get involved to make things better for society
53.3%—It is my CHOICE to get involved to make things better for society
 4.3%—Depends/Both/Neither
 2.1%—Don't Know

"Which of the following reasons BEST describes why you would choose to vote in elections?"

30.3%—Because voting is my responsibility as a citizen
26.9%—Because my vote, along with others, can affect the outcome of the election
33.8%—Because my vote is an expression of my choice
 6.7%—Don't know
 2.3%—Refused

"Now I'm going to read you some pairs of statements to see how you feel about some matters. Please tell me which you agree with more, even if neither is exactly how you feel."

39.4%—Most of the time people try to be helpful
54.7%—Most of the time people are just looking out for themselves
 3.9%—Depends/Both/Neither
 1.6%—Don't know

Source: The 2006 Civic and Political Health of the Nation Survey at http://www.pewtrusts.org/our_work_report_detail.aspx?id=19762.

said they voted because it "is the expression of my choice" than said they voted because it "is my responsibility as a citizen" (30.3 percent). These results reflect similar findings from a more recent 2010 survey from the Center for the Constitution at James Madison's Montpelier. In that survey respondents were asked to name their top- and second-highest reason for why they would vote. "To express my support for a candidate or issue" was the top reason, followed by "Because it is my civic duty." When comparing answers by age, younger Americans (those aged 18–24) are decidedly not motivated by a sense of civic duty. "I don't vote" was tied with "To express support for a candidate or issue" among younger respondents. "Because it is my civic duty" ranked as the fourth-highest reason for why a younger person would vote.[3]

Americans report being more motivated to civic participation out of a sense of self-interest; they also do not think they are alone. Respondents to the 2006 Civic and Political Health Survey were asked about the primary motivations of others. A clear majority (55 percent) agreed with the statement, "Most of the time people are just looking out for themselves" with only 39 percent agreeing, "Most of the time people try to be helpful."[4]

These data plainly suggests that the motivations for individuals to participate in the civic life of America today are not dominated by a sense of civic duty. There is a clear tilt toward the self-interest motivation, and the declining rates of traditional forms of civic and political participation, which have caused considerable alarm in recent years, reflect some of the consequences of that changed calculus for participation.

WHY IS CIVIC DUTY MOTIVATION IMPORTANT?

This tilt in favor of self-interest motivation and against civic duty motivation is important to understand because it has implications for the health of American society, both political and nonpolitical. For our purpose, we can best see these health implications through the lens of social capital. Social capital simply refers to the value that comes from social networks of people. The sociologist James Coleman described social capital as social structures that facilitate the actions of actors operating within these structures. Social capital makes it possible for actors to collectively achieve ends via social structures that would not be possible to achieve absent the social structures (1988, S98). Robert Putnam, describing social capital as the "social networks and the norms of reciprocity and trustworthiness that arise from them" points out that a society full of virtuous individuals who are also socially isolated from one another is not necessarily a society rich in social capital (2000, 19).

Putnam characterizes social capital as a producer of civic participation and links it to civic health in several ways. First, social capital makes it easier for a society to solve collective problems. The more social capital in a society, that is, the more there are social networks, norms of reciprocity, and trust, the easier it will be for people in that society to cooperate with one another to work on solving problems. Second, social capital makes virtually every transaction in a community, from economic to social, advance more smoothly because repeated transactions would have produced a reservoir of trust. Third, social capital makes us more aware of each other and each other's problems, and ultimately more tolerant of each other (2000, 288–89).

However, as Mutz (2006) has found, because contemporary life is organized so much around self-interest, a highly participatory democracy is increasingly at odds with a highly deliberative democracy. Americans who are most knowledgeable about and interested in public affairs are also the least likely to be exposed to views that are contradictory to their own. Mutz argues that the idealized "good citizen" of American civic life (e.g., the citizen most knowledgeable, most engaged, and most interested) is also the citizen least likely to be exposed to any kind of political discussions or views that would differ markedly from their own. Why? Perhaps because for too many people the goal of associating and participating is not to increase one's understanding of others or other's views, but at best to have one's own views reinforced or at worst to impose one's views on others. This has implications for social capital because, as Mutz shows, when it comes to associational membership, membership in most voluntary associations (the places where social capital is created) is not related to increased exposure to crosscutting political discussion. In short, the tilt toward self-interest may even invade the creation of social capital, in that citizens self-select how they are exposed to other people, especially people who hold views different from their own.

As Levine notes, it is still vitally important for a society to have some people, some of the time who are "committed to the health of our civic institutions in a way that, if not perfectly neutral, is at least open-ended" (2007, 57). In his study of the civic motivations for voting, Campbell argues that voting as a specific and central act of citizens in a democratic society has profound civic consequences:

> *On the civic side, how many people vote reflect the nation's collective level of commitment to the responsibilities of citizenship in a participatory democracy. Voting has a communal dimension to it, thus triggering a concern that voter apathy impacts a whole that is greater than the sum of individual's interests. The level of voter participation is an important indicator of our electoral system's legitimacy. As turnout fall, that legitimacy is threatened.* (2006, 187)

American society needs to have people motivated by a sense of civic duty because of the civic health side effects it produces either in the form of social capital or the recognition that the civic whole is greater than the sum of individual's interest; without a certain level of civic health, some problems will simply be too difficult if not impossible for society to solve. It seems clear from this perspective that the extent to which civic participation is motivated more by self-interest and less by civic duty is the extent to which American society is potentially worse off.

DECLINES IN TRADITIONAL FORMS OF PARTICIPATION

Longitudinal evidence of most forms of traditional civic and political participation spanning the nation's history is not available. But, we do have available ample evidence concerning several of the most traditional civic and political activities over the last half century. From voting to joining community groups and associations, social and political commentators from across the ideological divide have noted and lamented that civic and political participation appears to have waned in the last half century. Evidence of the decline is briefly summarized here.

Voting

No act of citizenship, and no form of participation, is more important in a democracy than that of voting. Yet, the United States has always had a difficult relationship with voting, as we will read about later in Chapter 2. Voting turnout in presidential elections rose steadily from 1789 to 1840, when turnout reached 80 percent of eligible voters. The increased turnout was driven by the slow removal of property and wealth restrictions on franchise such that suffrage for white men was dramatically expanded and by the growth of political parties, which acted as mobilizing agents and helped to increase participation dramatically.

Between 1840 and 1896 turnout fluctuated between a high of 83 percent and a low of 70 percent. Political party competition during this time was intense, and parties came to more clearly define different regional, social, economic, and political agendas, and became much better agents of mobilization. From 1896 to 1924 turnout declined, and the decline is generally attributable to the reduction in party competition as a result of the further regional alignment of the political parties. Turnout increased from 1924 to 1960 due in part to the massive mobilization of the population around the war effort and the lack of competition precipitated by the large shift in support during the New Deal to Franklin D. Roosevelt and the Democrats.

Since 1960 there has been a steady decline in turnout, from a high in 1960 of 65 percent to a low in 1996 of 49 percent. While turnout has gone up in the last two presidential elections, to an estimated 59 percent in 2008, it is not clear whether the increased turnout is due to increased partisan mobilization over unpopular wars and a recession or a signal of something more. Either way, turnout in 2008 is still below that of the 1950s and most of the 1960s.

14

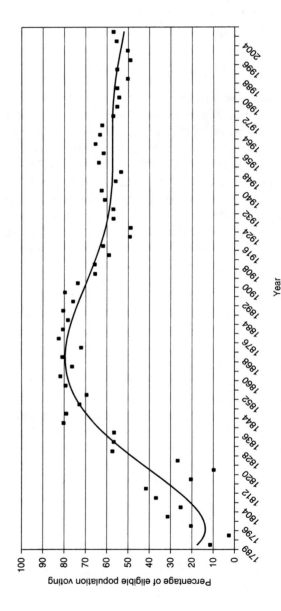

Figure 1.1 Trends in presidential voting, 1789–2008

Source: for 1789 to 1984: Walter Dean Burnham, 1987. "The Turnout Problem", in A. James Reichley, ed., Elections American Style. Washington, D.C.: Brookings Institution, pp. 113–114.

For 1988 to 2004: U.S. Census Bureau, Statistical Abstracts of the United States, Table 407. Participation in Elections for President and U.S. Representatives: 1932–2004.

This general decline has caused a great deal of concern because there are several reasons to have expected turnout to continue to improve rather than decline during this time. For one, informal and formal restrictions on political participation, in the South in particular, have largely been removed, and the voting age has been lowered from 21 years to 18 years. Both actions served to expand the eligible electorate. Second, access to education and educational attainment, which is strongly associated with increased voting at the individual level, has increased dramatically during this period.

Finally, procedural requirements related to registration have eased in large part due to federal legislation (e.g., the 1993 law known as "motor voter registration") making registration almost automatic when a citizen accesses certain government services such as applying for a driver's license or welfare services. Many explanations have been offered, from the decline in voter mobilization by political parties to increased prominence of television and replacement of the very engaged World War II generation with the less engaged Baby Boomer and GenXers (Teixeira 1992; Putnam 2000).

Associational Membership

Associations have been an important and distinctive part of American public life for as long as the country has existed, and even for some time before then (Schlesinger 1944). In *Democracy in America*, Tocqueville most famously described the unique role of associations in preindustrial America:

> The Americans make associations to give entertainments, to found seminaries, to build inns, to construct churches, to diffuse books, to send missionaries to the antipodes; they found in their manner hospitals, prisons, or schools. If it be proposed to inculcate some truth, or to foster some feeling by the encouragement of a great example, they form a society. Wherever, at the head of some new undertaking,

you see the government in France, or a man of rank in England, in the Untied States you will be sure to find an association. (1956 [1832], 198)

Tocqueville is describing a society where associational activities are pervasive, where the glue of society is the association, and where problems and initiatives from small to large are handled by associational activity.

However, as Skocpol and Putnam have shown, national chapter-based civic associations have been on the decline since the middle part of the twentieth century. These types of associations, what Putnam calls "face-to-face" associations, have dramatically declined in terms of both membership (the median peak year of membership of these associations is 1958.5) and importance in American civic and political life (Putnam 2000). They have been replaced by professionally managed citizens' associations and advocacy groups that are often centrally located in New York City or Washington, D.C. These professionally managed associations are far different from the mass-membership chapter-based associations in that they ask little of Americans (Skocpol 2003).

Tocqueville saw an America where individual citizens came together to handle problems small and large via associational activity. Today, with the pervasion of professionally managed associations and the decline in mass-membership chapter-based associations, Americans are asked only to give money—the new currency of the democratic way in America.

Church Membership and Attendance

Church membership and attendance has always been about much more than the spiritual in America.[5] What separates a religious institution from an association is the explicitly spiritual nature of the former. But, the participatory benefits to society are similar, and some commentators argue that faith communities are the single largest repository of social

Table 1.2 Peak membership year and rate for national civic associations

Name	Peak Year	Membership Rate at Peak Year Founded
4-H	1950	180,000
Ameircan Association of University Women	1955	53,000
American Bowling Congress	1964	83,000
American Leagion	1945	274,000
B'nai B'rith	1947	78,000
Boy and Girl Scouts adult leaders	1957	50,000
Boy Scouts and Girl Scouts	1972	156,000
Boy Scouts	1972	190,000
Girl Scouts	1969	125,000
Business Professional Women	1951	17,000
Eagles	1947	29,000
Order of the Eastern Star	1930	50,000
Elks	1970	25,000
General Federation of Women's Clubs	1956	16,000
Grange	1952	16,000
Hadassah	1983	123,000
Jaycees	1975	5,000
Kiwanis	1960	5,000
Knights of Columbus	1954	14,000
League of Women Voters	1965	2,000
Lions	1967	9,000
Masons	1927	90,000
Moose (male only)	1980	19,000
Moose (female only)	1990	6,000
NAACP	1944	31,000
Odd Fellows	1920	54,000
Optimists	1990	2,000
Parent-Teacher Association	1960	48,000
Red Cross Volunteers	1956	19,000
Rotary	1967	5,000
Shriners	1960	15,000
Veterans of Foreign Wars	1945	114,000
Women's Bowling Congress	1978	54,000
Women's Christian Temperance Union	1920	11,000
Median	**1958.5**	**30,000**

Source: Putnam, *Bowling Alone*, pp. 438–439.

capital in America (Putnam 2000). Regular church attendees have the opportunity to participate in the governance of the organization, help make decisions about charity and other church activities, organize and run meetings, engage in community outreach, and advocate for causes, both civic and political. The church is, in short, much like the voluntary association in that while it brings people together for explicitly spiritual reasons it also creates a situation where civic and political skills are honed. It is a very powerful civic and political participation incubator (Hougland and Christenson 1983; Verba, Schlozman, and Brady 1995; Djupe and Grant 2001).

However, like associational membership, church membership and attendance has been on the decline since the middle of the twentieth century. Aggregate longitudinal membership totals reported in the *Yearbook of American and Canadian Churches* show a decline in church membership from all-time highs in the late 1950s and early 1960s. The highest levels of membership were recorded in the early 1960s (1964, 1965, 1966, and 1968) at 65 percent of the population, with a steady drop-off from there. The lowest membership rates recorded since then were in 1999 and 2000, with 54 percent of the population reportedly members of a church, synagogue, or mosque in America.[6]

Church attendance follows a similar, although less dramatic pattern. Since 1939 The Gallup Poll has periodically asked respondents whether or not they have attended church or synagogue in the past seven days. The survey results show a high level of attendance in the mid- and late 1950s (1955 and 1958 at 49 percent) and a drop-off from there, with a low in 1996 (at 38 percent, a drop of 11 percentage points). The survey results also suggest sporadic church attendance from the 1980s to present, with year-to-year swings between 38 percent and 44 percent of respondents claiming to have attended church in the prior seven days. A reasonable assessment of the data suggests that church attendance has dropped from the high levels of attendance in the 1950s by as much as one-fifth.

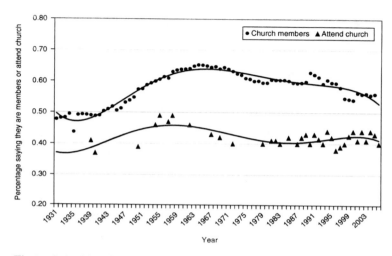

Figure 1.2 Trends in church membership and attendance, 1931–2006

Sources: Population: Table 2: Population, Housing Unites, Area Measurement, and Density: 1790–1990 at http://www.census.gov/population/censusdata/table-2.pdf

Church Membership: Eileen W. Lindner, ed., Yearbook of American and Canadian Churches, 2007 (Nashville: Abingdon Press, 2007), Table 1, p. 10

Church attendance: The Gallup Poll, varius years

Formula for extrapoliation between census counts: = (top# − bottom#)/(10) ∗ (cell-bottomyear) + bottom#

Nonvoting Political Activities

Voting, although by far the most important form of electoral political participation in a democracy is only one way in which citizens might participate in the democratic political process. Political voice can be expressed in a broad array of ways. Some of the most common forms of electoral participation other than voting include activities such as working for political campaigns, expressing political voice in ways such as wearing buttons and putting bumper stickers on cars, and attending political rallies and other political meetings. Electoral activities such as these are ones that exert high levels of pressure on elected officials, primarily because those officials want to either be elected or be reelected and thus need the support of those citizens actively participating (Verba, Schlozman, and

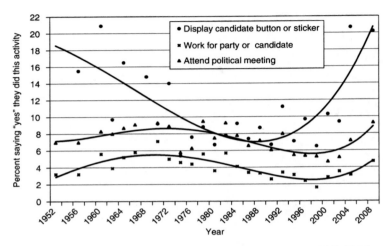

Figure 1.3   Trends in participation in political activities, 1952–2008
Source: American National Election Studies 1948–2008 Cumulative File.

Brady 1995). Indeed, even though voting rates are often used as a measure of the health of a democracy, one could hardly imagine calling America's democracy healthy if high voting rates were had at the expense of broad political participation. A healthy democracy would have both. Unfortunately, America has had neither in recent decades.

The American National Election Studies (ANES) has consistently asked respondents about certain types of nonvoting electoral participation since the early 1950s. In the past 50 years nonvoting electoral political participation has steadily declined. In terms of the costs involved, working for a political party or candidate is more costly than attending a political meeting, which is more costly than displaying a candidate button or sticker. Working for a political party or candidate requires time, knowledge, and self-confidence, for example, while attending a political meeting might require time and perhaps money depending upon the type of meeting. Regardless of the costs involved, participation has been on a steady decline with a slight upswing in the most recent elections. Working for a political party or candidate reached a high in 1970, but dropped to its lowest point in 1998.

In recent elections the rate has increased slightly, to just above 4 percent of the population, a level of participation that is still less than that of the high over the last half century.

Attending political meetings follows a similar pattern, reaching a modern high in 1978 and steadily declining to a modern day low in 2000 with an upswing in 2004 and 2008. The 2008 rate of 9 percent approaches the high rates of the late 1960s and early 1970s, but it is an open question as to whether this level of participation will remain high or drop again. The least costly activity, displaying a campaign button or sticker, has also similarly declined since the 1960s and early 1970s, but has also increased at a greater rate during the 1990s than the other two activities. And, while just over 20 percent of Americans say that they displayed a campaign button or sticker in 2008, only time will tell whether the 2004 and 2008 election cycles are an anomaly among recent elections. Leaving the 2004 and 2008 elections out of this analysis, Americans are still less likely to display their electoral preferences today than they were in the 1960s. In sum, a reasonable assessment of the data suggests that

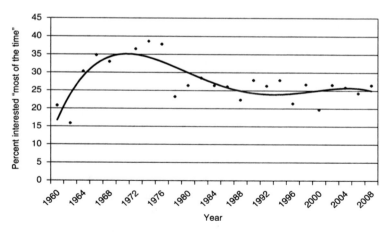

Figure 1.4 Trends in interest in public affairs, 1960–2008
Source: American National Election Study 1948–2008 Cumulative File
Percentage of respondents who say they are interested in public affairs most of the time (follow public affairs very closely for 1960 and 1962).

while recent election cycles have witnessed an upswing, the trends suggest that Americans are still less likely to engage in nonvoting electoral activities today than they were in the 1950s and 1960s.

From the perspective of normative democratic theory, high levels of civic and political participation would be unhealthy and unproductive (perhaps even counterproductive) if they were not accompanied by equally high levels of interest in and information about public affairs. In order for citizens to make quality judgments in a democratic political system, they must have quality information about the choices they have, and while quality information is dependent upon many factors, it is at least in part dependent upon the interest of the citizen to seek it out and study it. Thus, the act of following public affairs and staying informed is a participatory activity that results from interest. The ANES has asked respondents about their interest in public affairs since 1960. After rising through the 1960s and into the 1970s, interest in public affairs has dropped considerably since the 1970s. During the 1960s, an average of 29 percent of the population said they were interested in public affairs most of the time. That average went up to 34 percent during the 1970s, but dropped back down to around 25 percent in the 1980s, 1990s, and early 2000s. Indeed, in 2000, an average of 24 percent of the population said they were interested in public affairs most of the time. In addition, the surge in interest starting in the 1960s and carrying into the 1970s appears to have completely disappeared by the turn of the century. In 1964 only 16 percent of Americans said they were interested in public affairs most of the time. That percentage rose to just below 39 percent in 1974, but by 2008 had dropped back down to around 25 percent.

A reasonable assessment of the data suggests that interest in public affairs has dropped by around one-quarter since the 1970s. But more importantly, the fact that some indicators of political activity show an upswing in the last two presidential elections while interest in public affairs has been anemic suggests that the increased levels of political activity are not likely to be sustained beyond a period of hyper-partisan elections.

In sum, the last half century appears to be a period of general retrenchment in traditional forms of civic and political participation. While voting rates are up in the last two presidential elections, it is not clear whether those higher rates will be sustained. This is a question that also holds for other types of participation as well.

THE PARTICIPATION PUZZLE SO FAR

How can we explain these declines in civic participation? There is a sizeable body of scholarship that has focused on this question from several different perspectives. The dominant perspective is on the individual social and demographic characteristics of people such as age, education, and income, and is largely behavioral in orientation. Another perspective examines structures and rules and their role in participation, such as voter registration laws or the extent to which citizens are connected with political parties and other groups. A third is focused on social capital, or the connections people have with other people within and between social networks. A fourth focuses on new forms of participation and the generational differences in participation.

In their classic study of participation in America, Verba and Nie (1972) examined who participated in political activities and concluded that socioeconomic status strongly predicted participation in voting, campaign activities, and communal activities. People with higher levels of socioeconomic status, they demonstrated, developed civic attitudes that led to higher rates of participation. Wolfinger and Rosenstone also found a class bias in participation, concluding that while demographic factors such as age and income affected voting, the most powerful influence on voting is education (1980).

Teixeira (1992) expanded upon these basic findings in a study about why Americans did not vote, demonstrating that the costs of voting relative to the benefits gained from voting were too high for a large portion of the American electorate. In particular, nonvoters were more likely to be poorer, less educated, working class or blue collar, young, and racial minorities. Teixeira argued that while increasing the level of voting is important for democratic legitimacy and agenda setting, it would likely have no bearing on the outcome of elections. In an important study, Nie, Junn, and Stehlik-Barry (1996) looked at the relationship between education and participation and concluded that education is a primary cause of both political engagement (pursuing individual goals in the public sphere) and democratic citizenship (being generally involved for the public good). They argued that while increasing levels of formal education may not necessarily change the makeup or proportion of those who are politically engaged as opposed to those who are not, thus maintaining a certain class bias in the political system, it should broadly contribute to more democratic citizenship. Wattenberg (2002) confirmed the class bias in voting in an examination of voters and nonvoters, showing that those who are not very interested, not very partisan, not well educated, and not very old vote at much lower rates than otherwise is the case.

From the structural perspective, Piven and Cloward (1988) examined historical voter registration rules and the complexity of elections in the United States and concluded that they collectively discouraged voting. Just as the franchise was being expanded in the late 1800s, a series of legal changes effectively demobilized a large portion of working-class and poor voters. While the New Deal period saw some reverses in these trends, the structural barriers remained. They argue that intense competition for new voters in the early 1980s and an increased interest in registering poor and minority voters might finally reverse the barriers.

Rosenstone and Hansen (1993) expanded this perspective on low participation rates in a study of the role of political parties in mobilizing voters. They demonstrated the extent to which a lack of party mobilization was to blame for lower levels of voting and lower levels of participation in

•

nonvoting political and civic activities. Piven and Cloward (2000) picked up on the role of parties in a follow-up study to their influential 1988 study, arguing that the political parties had not taken advantage of the National Voter Registration Act of 1993 (known as the "Motor Voter" Act), which lifted some of the legal structural barriers to voter registration.

In a study that connected the individual and structural perspectives, Verba, Schlozman, and Brady (1995) examined the influence of resources and institutions on participation and developed a Civic Voluntarism Model to explain the causes of participation. They concluded, just as much of the earlier research had, that education plays a central role in participation, but additionally institutional affiliations such as membership in churches and unions provides important mobilizing influences on participation.

From the social capital perspective, Putnam's 1995 article and 2000 book, both titled *Bowling Alone*, brought the issue of declining rates of civic and political participation into the mainstream. In them, Putnam connects declining rates of civic and political participation with declining rates of structured, face-to-face organizations (such as participating in bowling leagues), what he called social capital. For Putnam the "connections among individuals—social networks and the norms of reciprocity and trustworthiness that arise from them" produced something akin to civic virtue. Without a healthy supply of social capital, he argued, society itself was in peril. What was replacing social capital, Putnam argued, were impersonal connections to large anonymous organizations on the national level and private family and entertainment on the individual level.

Putnam's study has led to a large body of research, much of it supportive but some of it also critical. Among the earliest and most persuasive critics was Ladd, who countered Putnam's data with evidence of his own and argued that "not even one set of systematic data support the thesis of 'Bowling Alone'" (1996, 1). Ladd demonstrated countertrends in group membership, voting, trust, parental involvement, and overall levels of civic participation (1996; 1999). Critics have also argued that the very indicators Putnam and others use to measure civic engagement and thus social capital are dated and do not reflect the new and varied ways in which Americans participate. Sanford (2007), for instance, takes exception to Putnam using traditional 1950s measures of civic and political engagement and defining social capital in terms of practices common prior to the widespread use of new technologies (such as television and the Internet). Sanford rhetorically asks whether changing definitions of what it means to be civic has resulted in a decline of civic life.

Perhaps the most important criticism of the social capital perspective, at least as far as this book is concerned, is that the causes identified lack any historical roots. Skocpol's criticism of Putnam's conclusions in *Bowling Alone* is instructive here. In *Diminished Democracy*, she argues that the primary focus of those attempting to understand civic decline in America has been on the choices that individual people make, but this focus says "far too little about the institutional and social causes at work" (2003, 175). Civic decline is likely not simply the result of television and the Internet. In addition, the other factors Putnam points to—the rise of two-income families, the loss of time and money, longer commutes—are themselves possibly caused by larger societal and political forces. At best the causal direction is unclear: it could be just as likely that the loss of time and money and the rise of two-income families are also the result of the same forces that caused the loss of social capital and subsequent drop in civic engagement. At minimum, they are intervening factors between the larger historical trends and institutional changes and social capital and civic participation. It is these larger trends and institutions that are the focus of this book.

A relatively recent perspective focuses on new forms of participation and younger citizens. For decades, scholars, pundits, and social commentators have noted the dramatic differences between the levels of civic and political partici- pation of younger adults and their elders. While there has been widespread concern about increasing disengagement among Americans generally, the levels of disengagement have been greatest among younger Americans. A typical examination of young adult participation is that of the first edition of Martin P. Wattenberg's *Is Voting for Young People?* (2007). Wattenberg focuses on the causes and conse- quences of the differences in levels of voting between young citizens and older citizens and recommends compulsory voting as the solution. In a subsequent edition, he includes a chapter examining new forms of civic engagement among young people.

The notion that young adults might be engaging differ- ently than their elders is the focus of a study by Zukin and his colleagues (2006). In it they demonstrate the different ways in which younger generations view citizen engagement and engage in political and civic participation. Zukin and his colleagues note the extent to which younger generations are less interested in traditional political participation, and view politics and political participation in far more negative terms than their elders, but are very engaged in civic activi- ties such as volunteering and solving community problems. Dalton's (2008) study of citizenship norms and younger generations argues that the traditional norms of citizenship, which encourage loyalty to and support for the traditional political order, are giving way to a new and differently engaged younger public that is less trusting of traditional politics, political institutions, and politicians but more sup- portive of democratic norms and principles.

While the literature on civic participation tells us much, what it tells us too little about are the larger societal-level forces and institutions that shape the environment within which citizens have been making the choices about whether and how to engage. What about the influence of societal changes over time? What about the influence of changing economic orientations over time? What about the historical conjunctures that set the institutional conditions within which people have made choices? What about the institutions of socialization? These questions are the focus of this book.

THE ROLE OF INSTITUTIONS IN CIVIC PARTICIPATION

In this book I use a historical institutional analytic framework to explore the broad questions about civic participation in America. I argue that the declining rates of civic and political participation seen over the last half century are visible symptoms of larger historical developments in several key societal-level institutions. As these important institutions have evolved, they have slowly altered both the self-interest and civic duty motivations for participation. In recent decades the civic duty motivation has given way almost completely to the self-interest motivation.

What are these important societal-level institutions and how have they changed? The first one is the institution of citizenship and the expansion of the franchise that over time has been accompanied by changes in the social and civic expectations of citizenship. Those changes came to emphasize citizen rights over citizen duties and obligations. As the franchise expanded, other institutions in society failed to adapt to the enlarged electorate in ways that helped newly enfranchised populations understand citizenship duties and obligations in addition to their citizenship rights. The second one is the institution of the nation's political economy and the development of an economic philosophy that came to focus almost singularly on individual (consumer) choice. The largely agrarian and trade-oriented political economy of early America gave way over time to a manufacturing and then consumer-oriented political economy. As this evolution in the nation's political economy took place, it resulted in a shifting of individual economic incentives away from a communitarian oriented civic virtue to a self-interested consumer-oriented one. Lost in the process was the spirit of public virtue and a concern for the common good in the political economy. The third one is the institution of the public sphere and government and the dramatic expansion in the size and scope of the national government that increasingly took problem solving out of the community and state and removed it to Washington. This evolution was driven by the demands citizens placed on government, but as the public sphere expanded and the national government's role in problem solving grew, it altered the calculus for civic participation, making more difficult "old-fashioned" civic engagement activities such as individual and community efforts and charities.

I argue that the historical changes in these three large-scale institutions fundamentally altered the motivations for participation and resulted in the general declines in civic and political participation that we have observed in the last half century. But, there is more to the story. I also examine the critical role in this alteration played by several institutions of civic socialization and contend that the three most important institutions of socialization, the family, school, and media, have not been able to mediate the negative influences on civic participation of these macro institutional changes.

My focus is on the whole forest, or at least large swaths of it, rather than individual trees or small stands of trees. My goal is very practical: to explore how the evolution of institutional spheres has affected the motivations of individuals to participate in the civic life of their country. I define institutions as do Hall and Taylor: the formal and informal procedures, routines, norms, and conventions embedded in the organizational structures of society (1996, 936). Influenced by scholars such as Parsons and Bellah, I think about institutions as normative in nature. In this way, institutions mediate social understandings about how we should act and what we should expect from others and from society. We learn these things in institutional contexts, both formal and informal. As Bellah et al. note, "Various institutional spheres—the economy, politics, the family, etc.—embody and specify culturally transmitted ultimate values in terms of what is right and wrong, good and bad. These normative patterns not only indicate the ends and purpose of our actions but also set limits to the means used, validating only those that are morally acceptable" (1991, 288).

Parsons' "prolegomena" on social institutions is concerned with the relationship of the individual to the institutions of society, and he contends that institutions are ultimately derived from values held in common by members of a community. The primary reason that an individual would obey an institutional norm is that the institutional norm carries some weight of moral authority over the individual rather than simply being a means to an end. Conformity to the institutional norm will continue "so far as [the individual] shares in the system of ultimate common value-attitudes of which the institutional system is a manifestation, and in so far as the former effectively governs his conduct" (1990, 326).

So, conformity to institutional norms is primarily a function of the shared nature of values expressed by those institutional norms. But when this primary function is lacking, Parsons contends that a secondary function of positive and negative sanctions can encourage conformity. Once established, "a system of institutional norms creates an interlocking of interests, both positive and negative, in its maintenance, and to a certain point its supports in the form of moral attachment may dissolve away and still leave it standing supported by the complex of interests, ultimately of sanctions since once positive interests are diverted from conformity only sanctions can take their place" (1990, 327).

However, there are limits to sanctions—whether positive or negative—because the strength of sanctions and the willingness to apply them are themselves a reflection of the moral authority directed toward the institutional norm by society. In the face of a changing institution, sanctions are likely to be difficult to impose because they would require a great deal of organization around a common set of ultimate values. If interlocking of interests is supposed to help maintain the institution, the very fact that the institutional sphere is evolving suggests that the interests might not have been well interlocked in the first place. The real question for us here is not whether society will apply sanctions to encourage particular kinds of behavior in relation to certain institutional norms, but how society responded to the evolution of norms in the institutional spheres of citizenship, the political economy, and government. What were the societal and political conditions that existed to establish the original procedures, routines, norms and conventions—the original institutions, and how did those procedures, routines, norms and conventions change? What societal and political conditions changed to cause the values held in common to change? Why were the institutions of socialization—the family, schools, and media—unable to mediate the evolution of norms in the institutions of citizenship, political economy, and government? Most importantly, how did these changes alter the motivations for civic participation?

Pierson and Skocpol (2002) outline three features of the historical institutional approach to studying political topics: that it addresses big questions that are inherently interesting to broad publics and fellow scholars; that it takes time seriously; and that it focuses on the macro context and examines the influences on both institutions and process in the macro context. This book satisfies all three features.

First, I am addressing a rather large and important issue concerning the American polity as it relates to the institutional influences on the calculus for participation in civic and political life. This issue is very important because, by the later part of the twentieth century, many of the legal and extra-legal barriers to participation in civic and political life had been lifted or were in the process of being lifted. In addition, while many of the informal barriers to participation still existed (and many still exist today), the trend has certainly been moving in a favorable direction to allow for increased, not decreased, participation. It is, in short, very puzzling that civic and political participation would drop rather than go up, and even though much attention has been given to this question at the individual level—it is a puzzle that has not yet been satisfactorily addressed at the societal level.

Second, I take history and historical forces seriously in attempting to address the topic. Using history as an analytic tool, I examine the role of institutional evolution and development in the drop in civic participation in America in the last half century, paying particular attention to the political, economic, societal, and legal forces that have influenced civic participation at a societal level. These forces developed over the course of the nation's history and collectively attained a critical mass some time after the 1950s.

Finally, my focus is on the interplay among institutions and their development over time, and ultimately upon the powerful disincentive those institutions have had on civic and political participation. In particular, I focus on the development of several societal institutions, particularly the changing rules of citizenship (and the particular emphasis on the rights of citizens over the duties of citizens), the transition of the American economy from one that emphasized the common good and collective governance to one that emphasizes the rights of individuals to make choices about what is or is not good for them (and the attendant disincentives to civic engagement), and the growth in the public sphere and the influence of the national government in community and state-level problem solving (and the attendant disincentives to local problem solving). I argue that the interplay between these societal institutions reached a critical threshold in the later part of the twentieth century and powerfully altered the incentives for citizen participation, and that the institutions that civically socialize us were not able to act as an effective countervailing force against these trends.

THE PLAN

This book has a very simple outline. Having laid out the context for the study, I turn next to the analysis. Chapters 2 to 4 each focus on a specific institution, tracing the historical development of that institution with an eye on explaining how the institution's development affected motivations for participation. Chapter 2 is on the institution of citizenship and examines how the expansion of citizenship rights—mainly via the right to vote—over time shifted the meaning of citizenship from one that involved duties and obligations to one that involved rights and benefits. This shift in the meaning of citizenship weakened the civic duty motivation for participation. Chapter 3 focuses on the institution of political economy and examines how the shift in the nation's political economy from its agrarian roots to its modern mass consumption base has altered the motivation for participation away from one rooted in agrarian civic duty toward one rooted in self-interested consumption. Chapter 4 focuses on the public sphere and the institution of government, and particularly on the activity level of the national government, and examines how, as the national government became more active and engaged in problem solving, the incentive for individual citizen engagement was reduced because the ability of individual citizens to be effective in their communities was made more difficult.

Chapter 5 focuses on the institution of civic socialization, and particularly on three agents of socialization, the family, school, and media. As the historical institutional changes converged between the 1950s and 1980s, the primary agents of socialization were themselves going through important changes that made it difficult for them to play an effective mediating role and to encourage the civic duty motivation for participation. The final chapter draws the four threads together and examines another period in our nation's history—the Progressive Era—where citizens revised and reinvented civic participation and created new forms of civic participation in response to social, economic, political, and cultural changes taking place at the time. I link those innovative and bold ways in which progressive reforms acted in the late nineteenth and early twentieth centuries to our current situation and argue that similarly innovative and bold ways of envisioning civic participation are needed today. I conclude by discussing the concept of civic entrepreneurship and argue that it holds promise as a possible way to link the civic duty and self-interest motivations together in a new form of civic participation for the twenty-first century.

I come about this work having been convinced that far more time and energy has been spent attempting to treat America's civic participation "dilemma" without a clear diagnosis of the problem. The goal of this book is therefore not necessarily to offer a specific treatment or set of treatments. While treatments are important and we certainly need them, it is beyond the scope of this project. Instead, the goal of this book is to offer a "big picture" diagnosis for how we have found ourselves where we are, and to expose the deep roots that explanation has in America's history and institutions. It is hoped that this enlarged view of the historical roots of America's contemporary participation puzzle may make the puzzle easier to understand, and therefore easier to treat.

CHAPTER 2

CITIZENSHIP AND CIVIC
PARTICIPATION

Photo 2.1   Statue of Aristotle
Aristotle explained that citizenship carried with it many obligations and duties
whose purpose was the good of the state and not the good of the individual.
Source: Photograph in the Carol M. Highsmith Archive. Library of Congress,
Prints and Photographs Division, LC-DIG-highsm-02522

Photo 2.2   Portrait of Elizabeth Cady Stanton
Elizabeth Cady Stanton was one of the leaders of the movement to grant women
full citizenship rights through suffrage.
Source: Prints & Photographs Division, Library of Congress, LC-USZ62-28195

The precise meaning of citizenship has been debated for thousands of years. While it has generally characterized membership in a common society, debates have persisted. What form should that membership take? Who should be allowed in, and who should be kept out? Those who were members already encouraged exclusivity and wished to place great barriers on access to citizenship. Being a citizen, they said, carried great duties and responsibilities that few in society could adequately shoulder. Those who were not members wished to broaden the scope so as to allow greater access to citizenship because being a citizen also brought with it many privileges and rights.

In practice, citizenship contributes to the public good and so the struggle over membership has been at least in part about how much marginal increase to the public good is to be gained by expanding membership. But the formula is also complicated by the fact that membership also brings with it individual political and social entitlements. Thus, citizenship describes membership in a common society and individual political and social benefits that membership brings. The most important individual political benefit, and the most important duty, that comes with citizenship in a democratic society is the vote. In this chapter I demonstrate that as the institution of citizenship expanded throughout American history, the incentive for civic participation shifted away from civic duty and toward self-interest.

From the founding of the republic to the present, citizenship has been a source of continuous struggle, but also a right that has expanded in scope. The source of the struggle was the contradiction between the principles of individual liberty upon which the nation was founded and the very narrow way in which citizenship was defined. Because the founding principles said that all men were self-evidently equal, and because this equality did not have to be earned but was instead an inherent part of humanity, once the practice of citizenship began to catch up with the principles of citizenship in America, the notion of citizenship as duty and obligation began to give way to the notion of citizenship as possession of privileges and rights. Once acquired, privileges and rights must be protected and expanded, and as a consequence the incentive for participation shifted toward self-interest.

Citizenship is not an incipient institutional sphere, and the emphasis the institution of citizenship has historically placed on the civic and moral commitment to society over self is not new either. However, this emphasis has evolved and given way to an equal or more important emphasis on self-interest, largely because other institutional spheres—namely education—have failed to transmit the importance of the value of civic duty over self-interest.

THE MEANING OF CITIZENSHIP

Although it is one of the oldest institutional spheres in Western thought, citizenship is not found in a single office, nor is it fully defined by the actions of a single person in society. Citizenship is very difficult to define, and broadly speaking what it represents has changed markedly over time (Barbalet 1988, 1; Rieseberg 1992, xvi). At its roots, citizenship dates to the Greeks, and in particular its enunciation in the *Politics*, where Aristotle explains that a citizen is a person who enjoys privileges and has obligations, who shares in the administration of the state and in the justice of the state, and whose purpose for doing these things is the good of the state rather than the good of the individual. The obligations that come with the status of citizen are several, including being called to military service and paying taxes. The privileges that a citizen has, according to Aristotle, are those related to participating in politics, holding office, and deliberating and helping decide important questions of the state (McKeon 1941, 1176–1182; Pocock 1995, 1–52).

Virtue is fundamental to citizenship for Aristotle, who says, "The good citizen . . . should know how to govern like a freeman, and how to obey like a freeman—these are the virtues of a citizen" (McKeon 1941, 1182). Thus, for Aristotle being a citizen was not something that just anyone could be. Because he viewed some people as naturally more virtuous than others, Aristotle thought that the obligations and benefits of citizenship fell to those who had virtue but not to those who lacked, because virtue would be required to serve the interests of the polis. And who had virtue? Virtue was found in the person who was free of any possible hindrances to his ability to serve the interests of the polis; in the person who was materially and socially free, and thus independent of mind. Any person who was not materially and socially free was not capable of being a citizen because that person was by definition not independent of mind either, and thus could not both assume the burdens of public life and subordinate private interests in carrying out those burdens (Ignatieff 1995, 55–57).

It makes a certain amount of sense: if citizenship comes with great responsibilities then only those who can fulfill the responsibilities *should* be citizens. All who were not materially and socially free (and by definition not independent of mind) were excluded from citizenship, such as slaves, women, non-Greeks, or casual residents who happened to be in the area. Thus, from the earliest thinking and writing about citizenship, two important points emerge: citizenship carries with it duties and responsibilities (that certainly also come with privileges, but even these privileges—the ability to participate in politics, hold office, and decide important questions of the state—sound a lot like heavy responsibilities) and only a few people have the ability to carry out those duties and responsibilities. This distinction between those capable of citizenship and those not capable of citizenship carried into Western civilization, and is clearly seen throughout history in European feudal society, where noblemen had much greater duties and rights than did common people.

There are other ways to think about citizenship. Another way is an idealized modern version of Aristotle's virtuous citizen, often referred to as an ideal republican citizen. An ideal republican citizen is a person who cares about the public: a person who has no interests beyond the common good and who pursues the common good with absolute devotion. The ideal republican citizen, essentially, has little or no private life because he has no room for private pursuits. Instead, he is absolutely virtuous in caring for and thinking about the rest of society, which is filled with people engaged in mostly private pursuits with little time or interest in public issues (Shklar 1991, 10–12).

These two ways of thinking about citizenship are rather exclusive in terms of who is considered worthy of or able to be a citizen. Only a select few can be called citizens by the standards of Aristotle or the ideal republican. However, another way to view citizenship, and one that is less exclusive, is to think about citizenship as membership in a nationality. In this sense, citizenship is a legal condition that comes with membership in a state, such as being American, Canadian, or Mexican, and that membership brings with it certain rights and privileges (Shklar 1991, 3–5).

Notice a shift here: citizenship as a legal condition brings with it rights and benefits, but says nothing about duties and obligations. Citizenship as a legal condition means that citizenship is granted to anyone who qualifies, regardless of whether they have the ability to share in the administration or justice of the state (as was required in Aristotle's definition) or whether they are concerned about the common good (as was the case in the ideal republican definition). Citizenship as a legal condition also says nothing about the quality of citizenship. A person does not have to do anything civic (such as vote) just because she is a legal citizen, and failing to vote will not endanger a person's rights and privileges. A citizen in this context could go her entire life and never express through action a concern about the common good. She might never vote, but would still be a full-fledged citizen.

However, a fourth way to think about citizenship is to apply some social and civic value to a person's civic activities. In other words, there are citizens and then there are "good" citizens. In this sense, a person might be considered a good citizen if they engage in civic activities and just a citizen (or even a "bad" citizen) if they do not engage in civic activities. For instance, a person might be considered a good citizen if he votes regularly and attends city council meetings and other types of public forums, and generally stays informed about issues of public importance. One who did none of these things would not reap the same social and civic praise (Shklar 1991, 5–10).

In America today the institutional sphere of citizenship is a combination of the last two ways of thinking about citizenship. It is a legal status that carries with it no formal obligations or duties other than to follow the law (which even noncitizens must do as well). But we also apply informal social value to people's activities. The reason we wear those "I voted" stickers on Election Day is so others will know we are good citizens who carried out our civic duty to vote.

An important question for any society, especially one where the conception of citizenship has dramatically evolved over the course of its history, is how to maintain the sense of duty and obligation among its citizens as the exclusivity of citizenship becomes less so. Among the most important institutional spheres in this regard are the educational institutions of society. But as we will see, while the ranks of the franchises grew to encompass more and more of the population, America's institutional capacity to civically incorporate and educate those newly full-fledged citizens struggled. The result has been an increasingly one-sided perspective of how individuals viewed their citizenship, a balance that favored citizenship as a legal condition with a dose (at times heavier and at times lighter) of kudos applied to behaviors and activities associated with good citizenship.

THE SLOW EXPANSION OF CITIZENSHIP AND THE SLOW DISAPPEARANCE OF CIVIC RESPONSIBILITY

Despite the high-minded rhetoric found in the Declaration of Independence and the U.S. Constitution, citizenship has been a difficult discussion for America, one filled with great tension. The tension, as Shklar so aptly described it, has been "between an acknowledged ideology of equal political rights and a deep and common desire to exclude and reject large groups of human beings from citizenship . . . " (1991, 28). In a democratic society whose most important document begins with *We The People*, the most fundamental right of citizenship is the act of voting, and indeed, to deny someone the right to vote is to deny their standing as a citizen (Shklar 1991, 3). It is this fundamental act that has been at the center of tension in America since its beginning.

When the framers gathered in Philadelphia to craft a new nation, they brought with them a legacy of restrictions on suffrage: in both England and the Colonies, voting was limited to property-owning adult men (Keyssar 2000, 5). This restriction was rooted in Aristotelian thinking about citizenship, that in the freeholders were found the virtues required of citizenship, and these virtues were not found in other classes of people (Williams 1960, 3). In addition, men of property were thought to have a unique stake in society and were thus thought to be more committed members of the community. They were also thought to be more sufficiently independent of influences that might limit their range of free choice (Keyssar 2000, 5). Novak argues that the idea of suffrage, and thus real standing as a citizen, was simply not discussed much in early America; it was not part of a positivistic legal and political language of early American thinkers and statesmen. Indeed, until the Civil War and the passage of the Fourteenth Amendment, status within society from which rights and duties flowed was very much regulated from the bottom up via the particular regulations and policies of associational memberships, institutional affiliations, and jurisdictional rules (2003, 90–105).

Yet, the seeds of tension had been sown long before the passage of the Fourteenth Amendment. The revolution itself had undermined the idea of virtual representation. The Colonies rejected the idea that virtual representation in Parliament was as good as actual representation. The idea that the legitimacy of government rested upon the consent of the governed became a central part of American political thought and so, too, the Lockean notion of natural rights and equality. Indeed, individual rights and liberties—ideas upon which the new nation was created—formed the foundation for thinking about citizenship in terms of rights and privileges. Thus, the values and principles at the heart of the revolution became increasingly difficult to square with the actual practices of denying the right to vote to so many people (Keyssar 2000, 25). Because of this, a large part of American history has been focused on efforts to expand suffrage and civil rights generally. The institution of citizenship has continuously evolved: the removal of property and tax qualifications for white males, the end of slavery (and granting former slaves the rights of citizenship) at the end of the Civil War, the granting of suffrage to women, and the federal enforcement of voting rights and civil rights of African Americans, especially in the South, in the 1960s. In each case, public standing as a citizen was the goal. The notion of individual rights and equality, and simple fairness, was the argument, and fundamental to the development of this argument has been the evolution of voting as a right of citizenship rather than a duty or obligation of citizenship.

A brief examination of the social and political movements to expand suffrage, first to all white men when property requirements were removed and finally to young adults in the early 1970s, allows us to see the evolution of the institution of citizenship. There is quite a distance from Chancellor James Kent's extolling the incorruptible virtue of free and independent lords of the soil in defending New York's freehold suffrage requirements in the 1820s to President Lyndon Johnson's reprimanding a joint session of Congress in front of a prime-time national television audience in 1965 by saying, "It is wrong—deadly wrong—to deny any of your fellow Americans the right to vote in this country" (Chute 1960, 297; Lawson 1976, 312).

This brief examination allows us to see something else about voting as well: it loses its value as a right of citizenship the more universally it is granted, and this alters the calculus of motivation away from civic duty and toward self-interest. As Shklar so aptly noted, it was the denial of suffrage that made it so valuable. If the right to vote was a mark of standing—of citizenship—then any group of people who desired the equal standing that citizenship brought with it desired the right to vote. Once acquired, the right to vote "conferred no other personal advantages. Not the exercise, only the right, signified deeply" (1991, 27). Thus, the value of suffrage was a function of its limited distribution in society. The practical goal—the right to vote—was an important function of the moral goal, equality of citizenship. By the early 1970s, suffrage in America was universal, and if the number of citizens engaging in the act of voting is any indication, its practical value was far less important than its moral value.

PROPERTY AND THE GRANT OF CITIZENSHIP

The American Revolution, as Keyssar argues, produced only modest gains in the formal democratization of politics

(2000, 24). While there surely was an appreciable difference in the number of adult men who could vote after the war than before it, the political elite were divided on the question of universal adult male suffrage and the role of property ownership. Thomas Jefferson was among the group of the political elite who envisioned a broad grant of suffrage. His views were often at odds with the majority of the elite, however. For instance, in his *Notes on the State of Virginia*, Jefferson made a list of grievances with the Virginia constitution of 1776. Having been in France at the time it was written, Jefferson was not able to have the kind of influence over it that he would like to have had. Of the list of defects he noted in that constitution, the number one was that it granted suffrage only to freeholders and did not grant suffrage to those men who "pay and fight for its support" who he argued were "unrepresented in the legislature" (1954, 118). In his draft of the Northwest Ordinance of 1784, Jefferson proposed a legislative body to govern the territories that would be selected by an electorate made up of all adult males, which was as broad a grant of suffrage as that seen anywhere in the world at the time (Ford 1904–1905, 118). This was rejected, and replaced instead with a 50-acre freehold qualification for voting (Williams 1960, 117).

At the Federal Convention of 1787, supporters of universal male suffrage argued that it was anathema to the philosophy of the revolution itself not to allow for a broad grant of suffrage. Referencing the revolutionary slogan, "no taxation without representation," Oliver Ellsworth wondered how those who opposed a broad grant of suffrage could hold the seemingly contradictory views they held (Farrand 1966, 202).

But opponents still clung to the centuries-old view that virtue was to be found in the propertied class of people, and opposed granting suffrage too broadly because it would empower common people who lacked the virtues needed to make dispassionate decisions. Gouverneur Morris worried that the main danger to the new country came from the democratic elements of the constitution. He specifically worried that if given the vote, people with no property would simply sell their votes to the rich. This view was shared by many at the convention (Farrand 1966, 202–209). Because they could not agree, the issue of suffrage was left to the states, linking the franchise in national elections to state suffrage laws. This was, like so many acts of the Federal Convention, a compromise that shifted debate to the states. Nevertheless, the idea that something was not right—that the values and principles at the heart of the revolution were somehow not expressed in suffrage laws and that all people had the right to political equality—was there and would not go away.

States addressed the suffrage question in different ways, but by the middle of the nineteenth century, universal male suffrage was the law in most of them. There is no one factor that can account for the removal of property requirements at the state level, but as Keyssar notes, the changes were spawned by a convergence of different factors. Among these were the widespread changes in the social structure and social composition of the nation's population, brought on by the increasingly manufacturing-oriented economy, the needs of the enfranchised classes to protect their positions by expanding their ranks, and political party competition for new voters (2000, 33–42).

However, the one constant thread was the demand by reformers for rights rooted in the democratic principles of liberty and equality. The idea that the right to vote as a central act of citizenship was a natural right rather than a recognition of some virtue or higher reasoning ability conveyed by ownership of land was becoming an increasingly commonly held view. Some called the property test an irrational prejudice (Keyssar 2000, 43), whereas others such as Lucas P. Thompson, a reformer from Amherst Virginia, wondered sarcastically what the ownership of land brought with it: "I think it will prove that his favourite freehold test, is not quite so good as [people seem] to think, unless there be something in the ownership of land, that by enchantment or magic converts frail erring men, into infallible and impeccable beings" (Peterson 1966, 403).

Despite the high-minded rhetoric of reformers, linking the end of the freehold requirements to democratic principles, individual liberties, and natural rights, the reality of the reforms looked less than the reformer's language implied. While reformers called their victories "universal suffrage," it was in reality suffrage for white men only, leaving the majority of Americans still without the right to vote. Indeed, some of the reformers who worked so hard to expand suffrage to white men held far different views when it came to suffrage for blacks and women (Chute 1960, 311–316). For many white men, the right to vote was a stamp of full recognition as a citizen and once gained, the urgency of reform seemed less important than it had been.

FROM SLAVERY TO CITIZENSHIP

The civic status of blacks during the revolutionary period was mixed, with some states granting property-owning blacks the vote and other states denying it. However, as the right to vote was expanded from property-owning men to all men throughout the early nineteenth century, suffrage was restricted for free and property-owning black men (women were never considered when it came to voting rights at this time). Indeed, the civic status of free and property-owning blacks moved in the opposite direction of that of white men in general (Berlin 1974, 48–50; Foner 1983, 206–207). Even alien whites were granted citizenship rights at the very time that blacks were being disenfranchised. There are many reasons for these counter trends, but central to them is a belief that blacks were a "lower race" and the fear of a black uprising (Smith 1997, 174–181 & 215).

The idea that blacks were a "lower race" fed directly into the argument that they could not carry out the duties and responsibilities of citizenship. Speaking to the New York Convention of 1821 on the issue of suffrage for blacks, John Z. Ross argued that "[blacks] are a peculiar people, incapable . . . of exercising that privilege with any sort of discretion, prudence, or independence. They have no just conception of civil liberty. They know not how to appreciate it, and are consequently indifferent to its preservation" (Peterson 1966, 215). The rebellion that led to a black republic in Haiti as well as Gabriel Prosser's insurrection in Virginia in 1800 and Denmark Vesey's Charleston conspiracy in 1821, added to white anxiety across the country about black civil status (Smith 1997, 178).

Yet, many thousands of ordinary people had been agitating for an end to slavery and an immediate emancipation of slaves for decades, and their interests in emancipation were revived in large part by great political, social, and religious transformations taking place across the United States in the 1820s and 1830s. On the religious front, a revival was sweeping the country that rejected Calvinistic beliefs in original sin and the damnation of humanity. Led by people like Charles Finney, the Calvinistic impulse toward salvation was turned on its head. Instead of salvation being the end of faith, Finney and others argued that salvation led to a new life, where one could focus on benevolent activities and care for other human beings. At a social level, this spiritual revival led to an impulse for social reform and coupled with the Jacksonian Democrats' desire to broaden the public's participation in politics, to an abolitionists' movement against slavery (Barnes 1964, ch. 1).

The Abolitionist Movement was very much a grassroots movement of egalitarian Christians who were socially and politically engaged by the black protests, rather than a movement of the political class. For example, the great abolitionist William Lloyd Garrison, who edited the abolitionist newspaper *The Liberator*, grew up poor and discovered the horrors of slavery after boarding with freed slaves in Baltimore (Cain 1995, 15). The primary vehicle for civic engagement was the church and other religious organizations such as the Society of Friends. The message was simple, as Elizur Wright, Jr., described it in 1833: "It is the duty of the holders of slaves to restore them to their liberty, and to extend to them the full protection of the law" (Stewart 1976, 44).

As far as abolitionists were concerned, slaves had rights and those rights were being denied. Yet, even as the Abolitionist Movement gained momentum, successes did not follow. By the outbreak of the Civil War, only five Northern states allowed blacks to vote on the same terms as whites, and blacks in Southern states found what little legal rights they had evaporating. Black Codes imposed special restrictions and punishments on both free blacks and slaves, and courts in both the North and the South limited or denied outright black citizenship, a practice that was affirmed by the 1857 Dred Scott case (Foner 1990, 58; Smith 1997, 253–271).

If the passage of the Thirteenth Amendment settled the question of slavery for good in America, the Fourteenth Amendment tried to settle the debate that had waged for nearly a century over who was and was not a citizen. The Fourteenth Amendment declared, "All persons born or naturalized in the United States, and subject to the jurisdiction thereof, are citizens of the United States and of the State wherein they reside." The broad language challenged legal discrimination across the country, but it did not guarantee freed slaves or anyone else the right to vote; that would take the Fifteenth Amendment. However, the broad language of the Fifteenth Amendment provided the avenue through which most Southern black men would be disenfranchised once again, this time via such measures as poll taxes and literacy tests.

For blacks across the country, but in the South especially, post–Civil War enfranchisement was a critical statement about their standing in society, and with the help of federal troops some 700,000 were registered to vote, and they turned out to vote as well, electing black leaders to seats in state legislatures and statewide offices across the South. Twenty southern blacks were elected to the U.S. House of Representatives and two to the U.S. Senate (Franklin 1961, 80; Franklin 1967, 319–320).

Yet, whites in the South never accepted black voting, and engaged in intimidation and violence to stop it. Black voters increasingly found it difficult to cast ballots, and their votes were increasingly not counted when they did manage to cast them. When Reconstruction came to an end with the Compromise of 1877, Southerners began to exclude black voters by all means possible, including laws requiring long residency and short registration periods, the payment of taxes, literacy tests, and the closing and relocating of polling locations, among others. In addition, whites also engaged in violent campaigns via the Ku Klux Klan to murder, hurt, and intimidate any blacks that might try to vote or hold office. Within a couple of decades, the number of black voters was reduced by half (Lawson 1976, 6; Foner 1990, 62–63; Smith 1997, 383–385; Keyssar 2000, 105–116). Black standing in society was once again less than equal.

The reactionary activities of Southern whites in the post-Reconstruction South were validated by the 1896 Supreme Court decision in *Plessy v. Ferguson*, where the doctrine of separate equality was enshrined in law. For decades, blacks were denied equal standings as citizens across the South, and were all but absent from politics until the Civil Rights Movement of the 1950s and 1960s. It was during those decades that, as Keyssar describes it, "a determined movement of African Americans stared down the threat of violence and reprisals to force the issue of voting rights into the public eye" (2000, 256). While the streets of the South were increasingly filled with thousands of protesters demanding the right to vote for blacks, much of the "official" struggle took place in the courts, and was slow. However, civil rights acts passed by Congress in 1957, 1960, and 1964, which had been subsequently litigated in the courts, suggested that the courts were no longer inclined to impede the protection of black voting (Grofman et al. 1992, 15–16).

The passage of the 1965 Voting Rights Act was a milestone politically, in that it finally committed the federal government to enforce the Fifteenth Amendment guaranteeing the right to vote to all citizens, but particularly to African Americans in the South who had been denied that right for nearly two centuries. As important was the symbolic message sent by the passage of the Act, and the federal government's aggressive enforcement of it across the South. African Americans, the Act said and the actions of the federal government indicated, were equal citizens.

WOMEN'S CITIZENSHIP THROUGH SUFFRAGE

While the civic status of free and property-owning black men was debatable during the revolutionary period, the civic status of women was not even questioned. As Buhl and Buhl have noted, the founders "had been more concerned with their sons than with their wives or daughters in the definition of citizenship" (2005, 3). The idea of women voting was so alien to the founders that the issue never came up, in public anyway. The founders shared assumptions about women and politics and public life so fully that they did not even need to debate them (Kerber 1995, 24). These assumptions are perhaps best characterized by the views of John Adams who, in a letter to James Sullivan in May 1776, argued that it would be too easy to go too far in granting suffrage to women (and others), and so it was best not to bring the subject up at all. As for women, Adams argued that if they were granted the right to vote, it would simply result in two votes for husbands, or the landlords or employers of women. Women were simply incapable of independent thought and action on such weighty issues "because their delicacy renders them unfit for practice and experience in the great business of life, and the hardy enterprise of war, as well as the arduous cares of state. Besides, their attention is so much engaged with the necessary nurture of their children that nature has made them fittist for domestic care" (Taylor et al. 1977, vol. 4, 208–213).

The origins of the women's suffrage movement can be traced to the antislavery movement in the 1830s. Indeed, in joining the antislavery movement, early women's activists attacked the notion that women were too delicate to contemplate the weighty issues of politics. Speaking at the Second National Anti-Slavery Convention of American

Women in Philadelphia in 1838, Sarah T. Smith argued that it was appropriate for women to discuss the subject of slavery because slavery was not merely a political question, but also "a question of justice, of humanity, of morality, of religion; a question which, while it involves considerations of immense importance to the welfare and prosperity of our country, enters deeply into the home" (Stanton et al. 1970, vol. 1, 339–341).

Women's rights activists saw the emancipation of slaves and the civic status of women as parts of the same goal: the realization of republican citizenship as envisioned by the American Revolution. The abolitionist movement gave women their first exposure to politics. By the 1840s, the women's rights movement was an important and well organized reform movement in its own right. By 1851, at the Second National Convention, women were placing suffrage at the "cornerstone of this enterprise" (Stanton et al. 1970, vol. 1, 825–826).

Yet, at the end of the Civil War when the Fourteenth and Fifteenth Amendments were passed, the civil status of women seemed to take a step back. Not only was there widespread resistance to granting equal citizenship status to women, but black abolitionist leaders such as Frederick Douglass and Wendell Phillips began to separate the issues of black enfranchisement from women's suffrage. The Fourteenth Amendment condoned the exclusion of women from voting by penalizing states only for excluding male inhabitants from voting. The Fifteenth Amendment protected the right of citizens to vote and only prohibited states and the federal government from abridging voting rights "on account of race, color, or previous condition of servitude," but not sex.

The result was a divided woman's suffrage movement, with one part forming the National Woman Suffrage Association and the other part forming the American Woman Suffrage Association. The National Woman Suffrage Association, led by Elizabeth Cady Stanton, Isabella Beecher Hooker, and Matilda Joslyn Gage, took a more radical tone, declaring the Republican and Democratic Parties corrupt, and calling for a new People's Party that would seek "the enfranchisement of woman" and the creation of a "political revolution [to] secure justice, liberty, and equality to every citizen of the United States" (Stanton et al. 1970, vol. 1, 516–520). Others took different approaches: Victoria Woodhull petitioned the House of Representatives, arguing that women were already enfranchised under the Fourteenth and Fifteenth Amendments, while Virginia L. Minor and Susan B. Anthony filed suits (Stanton et al. 1970, vol. 1, 443–489).

After several years of splintered efforts and failures, the woman's suffrage movement began to change for the better. Under the leadership of Carrie Chapman Catt and others, the movement became more organized, and by 1910 it became a mass movement as the result of the convergence of working-class interests in suffrage and the woman's suffrage movement's interest in the working class (Keyssar 2000, 206). In 1910 Arizona and Washington enfranchised women, and President Howard H. Taft spoke at the National American Woman Suffrage Association annual convention. In 1912 the Progressive Party endorsed women's right to vote. Between 1913 and 1918, seven states, including New York, enfranchised women, and so did Great Britain and several provinces of Canada.

But, it was World War I that provided the force needed to get a constitutional amendment passed. The war exposed a hypocrisy that few could ignore. In justifying the U.S. entry into the war, President Woodrow Wilson argued that the United States was fighting for democratic principles and for the rights of people to have a voice in their own governments. Suffragettes pointed out that they were sacrificing for something they did not have, and Wilson responded in 1918 by calling for a federal suffrage amendment as a "war measure." Addressing the Senate, Wilson said, "We have made partners of the women in this war. Shall we admit them only to a partnership of sacrifice and suffering and toll and not to a partnership of privilege and of right?" (Keyssar 2000, 216).

When Tennessee became the thirty-sixth state to ratify the amendment on August 18, 1920, women across America became full-fledged citizens. Abby Crawford Milton reflected on the moment it happened in a letter to Carrie Chapman Catt, "I shall never be as thrilled by the turn of any event as I was at the moment when the roll call that settled the citizenship of American women was heard" (Sims 1995, 350).

CITIZENSHIP RIGHTS FOR YOUNG AMERICANS

Unlike the civil rights movement or the movement for voting rights for women, little mass movement accompanied the drive to expand voting rights to 18-to-20-year-olds. While many young people may have wanted the right to vote, few ever found themselves in the streets demanding it. In addition, the period in which society "debated" whether or not to extend the vote to 18-year-olds was shorter than any prior debate about expanding citizenship rights. The requirement of property and income qualifications was gradually removed, over seventy years, so that by the time of the Civil War only Rhode Island retained a property requirement for voting (Peirce 1968, 206). It took just over 130 years for women to gain the right to vote, and it took around 100 years after the Civil War for African Americans to gain full legal access to the voting booth.

By contrast, it took just under 30 years for youth to gain the right to vote, and the primary force behind the effort was war. While there had been proposals to lower the voting age as far back as the nineteenth century, it was not until World War II that widespread momentum developed to expand suffrage down. When President Franklin D. Roosevelt signed the legislation lowering the draft age from 20 to 18 in 1942, Senator Harley Kilgore of West Virginia responded by introducing legislation to lower the voting age as well. Kilgore and others argued that people should not be asked to fight and die for a country in which they could not vote, adopting the slogan "old enough to fight, old enough to vote" (Kilgore 1943, 6).

The issue became important again during the Korean War. In 1954 President Dwight D. Eisenhower urged Congress in his State of the Union address to propose to the states a constitutional amendment lowering the voting age to 18 years, but no bill managed to make its way out of Congress. As many as 35 states also considered legislation during the 1950s, but only three states actually adopted measures lowering the voting age (Neale 1983, 6).

In the late 1960s, the United States was sending thousands of young people into an increasingly unpopular conflict in Vietnam. Frustration over Vietnam led to what little grassroots efforts there would ever be over the issue of youth voting. Several organizations, such as the Youth Franchise Coalition and Let Us Vote, were organized nationally to advocate for a constitutional amendment to lower the voting age. Let Us Vote's founder, Dennis Warren, echoed the arguments made by Senator Harley Kilgore during World War II in saying, "Young adults are accepting adult responsibilities and are qualified and willing to become politically active" (Cultrice 1992, 97–98).

In 1968 President Lyndon B. Johnson urged Congress to act, saying "it is time once more for Americans to measure the constraints of custom and tradition against the compelling force of reason and reality in regard to the test of age. The hour has come to take the next great step in the march of democracy. We should now extend the right to vote to more than ten million citizens unjustly denied that right" (Neale 1983, 8). After efforts to expand suffrage by amending the Voting Rights Act of 1965 were partially rejected by the U.S. Supreme Court in 1970, Senator Jennings Randolph of West Virginia introduced a constitutional amendment giving 18-year-olds the right to vote.

The process of approving the Twenty-sixth Amendment in the states took only two months and seven days, by far the fastest the states had ever approved a constitutional amendment. Upon ratification, President Richard M. Nixon urged newly enfranchised young citizens to exercise their rights saying they were "now fully included in the electoral process."[1] In the 1972 presidential election, the first in which they were eligible to vote, 51 percent of those aged 18–20 registered and actually voted, the highest turnout rate ever recorded for that age group. Since then, turnout rates have been as low as 32.5 percent in the 1996 presidential election (League of Women Voters of Cleveland Educational Fund 1999, 23).

The passage of the Twenty-sixth Amendment was important for two reasons. First, it marked the achievement of universal suffrage—universal citizenship rights—in the United States, almost 200 years after the founders declared their independence behind the words *We The People*. Second, while the fundamental argument for expanding voting rights to 18-year-olds was their service in war, the passage of the Twenty-sixth Amendment marked the first time in the American history that voting rights had been extended to a group of people in the absence of a large-scale social struggle for those rights. Indeed, by the late 1960s the idea of extending the fundamental rights of citizenship down to 18-year-olds came to be seen as a logical extension of the move to expand citizenship rights generally (Neale 1983, 3).

THE DIFFICULTY OF INSTITUTIONAL ADAPTATION: OLD CITIZENSHIP, NEW CITIZENSHIP AND THE MOTIVATION FOR PARTICIPATION

In historical terms, there have been two citizenships: the very limited Grecian notion of citizenship that was small-scale, culturally monolithic, hierarchical, discriminatory, required individual participation, and lasted from the time of the ancient Greeks to the French Revolution, and a second that is much more universal, culturally diverse, democratic, less discriminatory, requires little of individuals, and has been on the rise since the beginning of the eighteenth century (Riesenberg 1992, xviii–xix). In America, as the meaning of citizenship has evolved into this second meaning of citizenship, the motivation for participation has also shifted.

As Marshall explained, the second citizenship began to take hold first in England, and then in the American colonies and the rest of Europe. Marshall has divided the development of the second citizenship into three stages: civil, political, and social. The development of each stage coincides with an expanded view that citizenship comes with even more rights and benefits, but requires less civic duty (1950, 10).

The civil stage of citizenship is the stage where the full realization of liberty took hold, first in England during roughly the eighteenth century. Beginning with the Habeas Corpus Act of 1679 in England and running through the repeal of the Combination Act in 1824, civil rights were gradually granted to nearly all English people. These civil rights included freedom of speech, thought, and faith, and the right to own property, enter into contracts, and to receive due process of law—a right that made everyone equal in the eyes of the law. It is important to note that most of these civil rights did not bring with them any new or added obligations of citizenship: they were simply rights granted to people because they were citizens. In addition, many of these are the same rights that the American Founders put into their own constitution (the Bill of Rights) in 1791. The American Revolution was, in part, a product of the changing notion of citizenship that began in England in the early eighteenth century (Marshall 1950, 10–13).

The development of the political stage of citizenship took place roughly in the nineteenth century as the right to vote was gradually extended to more and more people. The principle for extending the right to vote to more people also changed, from one of economic substance (you could vote because you owned property) to one of personal status (you could vote because you had obtained some personal or legal status, such as reaching a certain age). In the United States, the full realization of suffrage happened in 1971, when the right to vote was extended to all people who have reached the age of 18. Again, by extending the right to vote based upon personal characteristics or legal status, citizenship was extended as well, but without any added obligations (Marshall 1950, 1–18).

Finally, the development of the social stage of citizenship, which overlaps to a great extent with the political stage of citizenship, takes place roughly in the twentieth century. Perhaps this overlap is the result of extending the franchise because in the twentieth century, as more and more people achieved the right to vote, the social rights of citizenship expanded as well, such as the right to earn a minimum wage and the right to free (and then compulsory) education (Marshall 1950, 18–27). In the United States, social rights are most easily seen today in the various antidiscrimination laws passed since the 1960s, or in equal employment opportunity statements saying that discrimination will not be tolerated based upon some social status factor such as race, age, or religious conviction.

Broadly speaking, then, citizenship today comes with privileges and rights that are, as Barbalet notes, found in the form of negative and positive obligations the state has to its citizens. On the one hand, the state is restricted in its ability to limit a citizen's civil rights; whereas on the other hand, the state is obligated to provide benefits in order for citizens to realize their social rights (1988, 20). Notice that, as we have discussed the development of citizenship from the Aristotelian view that it carried with it heavy duties and obligations and thus could only be granted to those who had the ability to carry out those heavy duties and obligations to the modern view that it comes with many privileges and rights, but few if any duties and obligations, the essence of citizenship itself has changed.

Observers call this "passive" or "private" citizenship because of the emphasis on rights and benefits and the absence of obligations (Kymlicka and Norman 1994, 352–381). Few Americans wake up in the morning and think about what their citizenship means, but if they did, even fewer would think about it in terms of participatory obligations and duties. Instead, most would probably think about it in terms of rights and privileges. This shift in the meaning and practice of citizenship has had a profound effect upon civic participation, encouraging the self-interested protection of rights and interests, while at the same time ignoring (and thus discouraging) participation out of a sense of civic duty.

As a mediator between the individual and society, institutions play a critical role in helping both individuals and society adapt to changes both are trying to deal with. As the franchise has expanded and the meaning of citizenship has changed, other institutions such as the institution of education have struggled to find an adequate mediating role. While we often confine "education" to a place where we go for several hours a day and formally learn, the educative task—the institution of education—has only recently taken on such a narrow conception. Indeed, when it comes to educating citizens we have a long history of thinking about education in a much broader way. For Aristotle, the laws and mores of the *Polis* educated people. Citizens deliberated on those laws and also lived under them. Thus, education for Aristotle was much more organic, and could never have been confined to a classroom. Bellah et al. characterize education in early America as closer "to what Aristotle imagined than what we have today. It was the whole community that educated: the home, the church, the voluntary association, and local politics had an educative function at least as important as that of the school" (1991, 147).

While the whole community educated, the founders also clearly understood the importance of education to the health and vitality of the new republic. In 1779 Thomas Jefferson proposed to the Virginia legislature a Bill for the More General Diffusion of Knowledge that was aimed at the general education of the citizenry so as to make them aware of their individual rights and to keep them vigilant against tyranny. As Pangle and Pangle (1993) note, while the bill was introduced into the Virginia legislature, it was, in typical Jefferson fashion, intended to serve as a model for the nation.

However, from the beginning of the nation, the institution of education, especially the formal school-based educational institutions, have confronted a dilemma (Butts 1978; 1980). As Jefferson argued, schools should educate for democratic citizenship. Citizens should understand and appreciate the important values of liberty, equality, justice, and the individual's obligation to the public good. For example, Elson found in her study of American schoolbooks of the nineteenth century, "The first duty of school book authors in their own eyes was to attach the child's loyalty to the state and nation. The sentiment of patriotism, love of country, vies with the love of God as the cornerstone of virtue: Patriotism . . . must be considered as the noblest of the social virtues" (1964, 282).

This approach has jousted with an increasingly dominant approach that stresses tradition and the notion of a national American identity and destiny, a devotion to individualism and free enterprise, and an attitude of superiority (Butts 1980). This approach leads to an institutional view that sees education's role as helping maximize individual human potential and that civic and social problems are primarily "technical rather than moral or political" (Bellah et al. 1991, 163).

We will deal more with this in Chapter 5, but suffice it to say here that the institution of education has struggled with this dilemma since the nation's founding. The result has been largely a failure to instill the values of civic duty such that, as the meaning of citizenship evolved and expanded, the motivation for participation evolved as well, away from civic duty and toward self-interest.

CONCLUSION

This chapter argues that citizenship rights and civic participation are linked in a broad institutional sphere, but in such a way as to favor self-interested participation. The expansion of the institution of citizenship has been a source of constant conflict in American history, and as that conflict has been settled over time, the responsibilities of citizenship have changed as well. The conflict has its roots in the founding of the country. On the one hand, the new nation claimed to be vastly different from anything that had come before it. America's founding documents said all men were equal, used the term *We The People* to describe those who wanted political freedom from Great Britain, and declared that all were endowed with certain natural rights, among them the right to life, liberty, and happiness. Yet, on the other hand, both citizenship and voting rights were initially defined very narrowly, and the result was that only property-tied men could exercise the fundamental right of citizenship and vote. This limited grant of citizenship and voting was rooted in ancient notions about where virtue was found, which kind of person was most responsible, and who had the most at stake in a political system. Thus, the values and principles of the new nation did not square with the reality of who was granted citizenship rights.

As a result of the limited grant of voting rights within the new political system, it became a very valuable right to have, and a significant thread of American political development has been the various efforts to expand citizenship rights, principally measured by suffrage, to all people. Initially, the focus was on the removal of property and tax qualifications for white men, but attention also turned to the ending of slavery and granting former slaves the rights of citizenship and then the granting of suffrage to women. Eventually, the federal government had to enforce voting rights and civil rights of African Americans, especially in the South, in the 1960s, and by the early 1970s the franchise was lowered from 21 to 18 without much mass social effort at all.

What got lost in the 200 year evolution of suffrage, what other institutions like education failed to mediate, was the importance of the notion of citizenship as carrying with it responsibilities and obligations. In most instances, the struggle for political and civil equality was based upon the founding principles and took the form of demanding the rights of citizenship as outlined in those principles. By the time that citizenship rights were universally granted and protected by the federal government, the notion of citizenship as duty and responsibility had given way nearly completely to the notion of citizenship as a right. This evolution tilted the scales toward the self-interest motivation for participation and away from the civic duty motivation for participation. As a right, citizenship carries with it no formal responsibilities or obligations, which leaves only socialization and informal social pressure to encourage voting.

CHAPTER 3

THE POLITICAL ECONOMY
OF CIVIC PARTICIPATION

Photo 3.1 Portrait of Alexander Hamilton
Alexander Hamilton argued that the nation's political economy should be organized to encourage the pursuit of private pursuits.
Source: Photograph of a mural by Constantino Brumidi in the United States Capitol, Washington. D.C. Prints & Photographs Division, Library of Congress, LC-DIG-det-4a26388

Photo 3.2   Portrait of Henry Ford
Henry Ford understood the consumer desires of people.
Source: National Photo Company Collection, Prints & Photographs Division,
Library of Congress, LC-USZ62-111278

The economy cannot be separated from the political process or the rest of society; as an institutional sphere the political economy is a fundamental part of the social and political whole. As such, the political economy plays a powerful role in encouraging or discouraging particular kinds of civic participation. For instance, Adam Smith believed that a political economy organized around competition in the free market would turn human greed and selfishness into a benefit for society by keeping prices low and making a variety of goods, products, and services available to people. Karl Marx believed that a political economy organized around the collective ownership of the means of production would lead to social conditions that would be beneficial to everyone in society equally. Civic participation would look vastly different under a Smithian political economy as compared to a Marxian political economy because the incentives for participation would be vastly different under each one.

The role that the political economy would play in encouraging civic participation was recognized by the founders of America from the very beginning of the nation's history, and that role was at the heart of an early disagreement between them. One group of founders, led by Thomas Jefferson, argued that the nation's political economy should be organized to encourage a public virtue that would cause citizens to focus on the needs of neighbor, community, and nation before their own self-interests. Another group of founders, led by Alexander Hamilton, argued that the nation's political economy should be organized to encourage citizens to engage in self-interested pursuits that would work toward and result in greater civic goals.

Initially, the nation's political economy favored the Jeffersonian approach because it was largely agrarian and trade oriented, and thus encouraged a communitarian-oriented civic virtue. However, as the nation's political economy evolved over time away from an agrarian economy and toward a manufacturing and then consumer-oriented economy, the incentives for participation changed. This evolution in the institution of political economy has resulted in a shift in the incentive for participation away from the civic duty and toward the self-interest. The Jeffersonian political economy does not exist in America today, even if the Jeffersonian ideals of civic virtue still have a hold on how we think about how and why citizens should be engaged.

In Pursuit of the Common Good

As a statement of principles, the Declaration of Independence was powerful, and many of its ideas, such as individual liberty, freedom and rights, political equality, rule of law, and limited government, found their way into the U.S. Constitution, the rules by which the new nation would operate. Granted, there was, as the Constitution clearly shows, a pragmatic side to the founders as well. They also built in checks on power just to make sure that if their idealism was misplaced, it would not lead again to the very tyranny they had fought to leave. There was also recognition, best expressed by James Madison in *Federalist 10* and *51,* that men did not always act in the common good but often did act in a self-interested way. Nevertheless, at the heart of the new political philosophy was a rethinking of the relationship between the people and government. This rethinking had it that the very purpose of government was the welfare of the people. It contrasted government under a monarch where, when set against their rulers, the interests of the people were usually common and contrary to those of the monarch. If the ruler was removed and the government's purpose and focus became "of the people, by the people, and for the people," then the aims of each—the government and the people—would be the same. Thus, in the new republic individual good and the common good would be organic . . . one and the same, and to deny the common good would be to deny the individual good (Wood 1969; Banning 1978).

But, how might a commitment to the common good be translated through time and ensured? Under a monarchical political system people's actions were governed by force or threat of force. But in a republican political system, force or threat of force could not be the driving agent of people's actions because this would be antithetical to this very system of governance: there should be no divergence of aims. To make matters even more difficult, the Constitution has a heavy emphasis on rights, which builds in a tension between the rights of individual people to be free and happy and the need for government to secure those rights. This tension is between obligations and rights, or between the common good and the individual good (Arendt 1963 [1990], 126–129). If America was going to become a new kind of state—one without a monarch—all of its citizens had to be committed to the common good. But, at the same time all citizens also had to be free to pursue their own private interests . . . or their happiness.

As an ideal, scholars think of the common good somewhat like we described ideal republican citizenship in the previous chapter. The ideal republican citizen was one who was concerned about the common good and had little or no private life. If one has little or no private life, however, then one has little or no interest in pursuing private goods. So, in practical terms, very few citizens could actually live as ideal republicans. Even the founders, who were the people most concerned about public affairs in America's early years, had many private pursuits. Thomas Jefferson loved his books, his farm, and his new university. George Washington owned thousands of acres of land, and this land made him a wealthy man. John Adams had many private business interests. In short, there were no ideal republican citizens in early America, even among the founders. The earliest citizens tried to balance the common good with private interests.

How, then, did the pursuit of the common good find expression in America if there were no ideal republican citizens to do it? The reigning philosophy of the time held that private citizens had a civic duty, and this civic duty was carried out by deliberating with each other about the common good and helping to shape the outcomes of that deliberation. In order to deliberate, citizens had to keep up with public affairs and be concerned about the whole community, and to take actions necessary to ensure the health and welfare of the whole community. This is known as the republican tradition in American politics, and it emphasized a concern for community and self-governance, while recognizing the fact that citizens would engage in self-interested behavior as well (Sandel 1996).

Another important question is how the relationship between public good and private good could be tilted slightly in favor of the public good without stamping out the opportunity for private interests or having an agent of force involved. The answer rested on the encouragement of public virtue. The new nation could not be one where individuals or groups were exclusively bent on private pursuits because things would quickly degenerate into anarchy.

Instead, much of how the nation would operate, including most importantly the nation's political economy, had to be oriented around the encouragement of a public spirit, a concern for the public good. A public spirit was a check on out of control self-interest (Banning, 1978; Nelson 1987).

For Jefferson and many others, this public virtue was found only in the political economy of the agrarian life of yeoman farmers, mechanics, and craftsmen, whom he called the "chosen people of God, if ever he had a chosen people, whose breasts he has made his peculiar deposit of substantial and genuine virtue." Economic independence bred virtue while economic dependence killed virtue and made corruption more likely. Jefferson argued, "Dependence begets subservience and venality, suffocates the germ of virtue, and prepares fit tools for the designs of ambition" (1954, 164–165). A manufacturing-based economy suffocated virtue because it made men dependent upon others for their existence, and such dependence made vice and corruption more likely, and vice and corruption were signs of self-interest not public good. Vice and corruption in the people would lead to vice and corruption in the government, and ultimately the aims of government would diverge from the aims of the people.

Jefferson, Madison, and others such as John Taylor supported economic policies that would encourage and support a civic-minded population. In particular, they believed in open trade so that excess American agriculture could be easily sold in the international markets and a continuous westward expansion would encourage the agrarian political economy, and thus the virtuous civically oriented citizen (Watts 1987). However, Jeffersonian republicanism was not a universally held view. Others, like Alexander Hamilton, argued for a more liberal political economy. Hamilton felt rather than organizing a political economy that would discourage private pursuits, the new nation should instead organize a political economy that would encourage private pursuits, which would ultimately work in the service of greater civic goals. In Hamilton's view, disinterested patriotic virtue was naïve. To achieve the republican aims of the revolution, Hamilton argued that a strong national economy built on a manufacturing base that would be respected around the world was needed. The result, he believed, would be a strong nation with proud citizens, whose pride in their nation would translate into civic commitment to their nation. Thus, for Hamilton, civic-minded citizenship could not be had by suppressing self-interest because the net result would be a weak nation both economically and civically. Instead, civic-minded citizenship would be had by encouraging self-interested behavior, especially economic self-interested behavior, and then harnessing the successes of that self-interested behavior to the benefit of the nation as a whole (Nelson 1987; Watts 1987; Sandel 1996).

The early debate between Jeffersonian republicans and Hamiltonian liberals over the new nation's political economy was thus a debate about what role the economy would play in influencing why and how citizens would participate in the civic and political life of the nation. And for a short period of time it looked as though Jeffersonian views would prevail. As president, Jefferson's most important action designed to achieve a lasting republican political economy was the Louisiana Purchase, which provided answers to the two pillars of a republican political economy that would promote and maintain a virtuous and civic-minded people: abundant land for an agricultural economy and access to the Mississippi River and New Orleans for export of excess products to the world (Malone 1970, chs. 3–5; McCoy 1980, 196–203).

AN EVOLVING POLITICAL ECONOMY AND EVOLVING MOTIVATIONS FOR PARTICIPATION

As Sandel notes, history often has the final word on debates within a society, and sometimes settles the debate so completely that few can remember ever having it (1996, 143). This is the case with the initial debate over the nation's political economy and the role it would play in encouraging and cultivating civic life in America. Whether the American economy would have a strong manufacturing base or not was a moot point by the middle of the nineteenth century. Within 50 years of the "revolution of 1800," the growth of the American economy reflected the strength of its industrial sector as did, in part, the growth of major cities such as Boston, New York, Philadelphia, and Baltimore (see North 1966, Part I).

The election of 1800, important for many reasons, did not in fact mark a dramatic shift toward a Jeffersonian republican political economy based upon agriculture and exports. Perhaps the die had been cast with the passage of the Tariff Act of 1789 that was designed to provide the government with an income not only to pay its debts, but also to encourage and protect domestic manufacturing. But in the end it was Jefferson and his fellow Democratic-Republican's acceptance of most of the financial system that Hamilton and the Federalists had put together that set the tone for America's political economy. While Democratic-Republicans continued to oppose the national bank, the Jefferson administration paid debt claims against the government that made borrowing the money for the Louisiana Purchase much easier. In addition, taxes collected from increased trade allowed the government to pay off its debt, and increased customs duties made it possible for President Jefferson to eliminate internal taxes. When the charter of the Bank of the United States expired, President Madison strongly supported its rechartering. While the agrarian economy remained strong and important, Jeffersonian republicanism and the political economy it advocated was forced to give much room to an increasingly powerful industrial economy, and an economy that shifted the civic balance, slightly at first but more dramatically in years to come, by encouraging self-interested behavior. This shift has continued, unabated, ever since. The effect on civic and political participation, over time, was to tilt the balance away from civic duty toward self-interest.

The shift to an industrial economy was subtle at first. As Ratner, Soltow and Sylla (1979, 183) note, the etymology of the term "manufacture" has its roots in Latin and refers to making things by hand. Early manufacturing in America has little resemblance to the kind conditions described by Upton Sinclair a century later in *The Jungle*. Early manufacturing was largely family or household-based. As Tench Coxe, the coauthor with Alexander Hamilton of the famous 1791 *Report on Manufactures*, noted in Lancaster and surrounding counties of Pennsylvania in 1786, nearly a third of all families were engaged in household manufacturing. In his "A View of the United States of America," Coxe produced a detailed census of the number of hatmakers, shoemakers, tanners, saddlers, tailors, weavers, white and black smiths, wheelwrights, coopers, watchmakers, dyers, gunsmiths, rope makers, tinners, nail makers, silversmiths, potters, brewers, and printers (in both English and German), and other household-based manufacturers in the midland counties of Pennsylvania (1794, 312–313).

While Jeffersonian republicans celebrated the virtue of the small farmer, they were not necessarily bothered by the mechanics, craftsmen, and other household-based manufacturers that Coxe described. Such household-based manufacturing did not concentrate men and machines in cities, far removed from the virtues of agrarian life where vice and corruption flourished and where civic-mindedness did not exist. Small household manufacturing also drew heavily upon the labor of women and children, leaving men to work the farms. Thus, the civic capacities so important to republicans that an agrarian and rural political economy encouraged were not necessarily threatened by household manufacturing (Sandel 1996, 144). Indeed, through the middle of the nineteenth century the civic virtue so important to Jeffersonian republicanism seemed intact. Writing in the 1830s, Tocqueville described how free institutions in America served to combat the evils of individualism. Individualism, Tocqueville argued, "At first, only saps the virtues of public life; but, in the long run, it attacks and destroys all others . . ." (1956 [1832], 193).

How did America combat the evils of individualism? Tocqueville's answer would have warmed Jefferson's heart, because Tocqueville contended that while private pursuits certainly directed many of the actions of a person's life, they were also often sacrificed to the public welfare. Americans had at the beginning of the nation's history attended to public interests out of necessity, but over time it had become a habit. Tocqueville saw in his tour of America people who accepted the duty of participation because they saw the institutions of society as their own, and they had the habit of engagement. "Men attend to the interests of the public, first by necessity, afterwards by choice: what was intentional becomes an instinct; and by dint of working for the good of one's fellow citizens, the habit and the taste for serving them is at length acquired" (Tocqueville 1956 [1832], 197).

FROM HOUSEHOLD MANUFACTURING TO THE INDUSTRIAL REVOLUTION

Thus, it would seem, almost half a century on, the civic values of Jeffersonian republicanism were being affirmed by Tocqueville, who reported that Americans, many of whom made their livings in agriculture or small household manufacturing, participated in the civic life of their communities and the nation out of a sense of duty, a sense that had become a habit. But within a few short years, the nation's political economy would fundamentally shift away from one dominated by agrarian and small household manufacturing to one equally composed of factories fully embracing the industrial revolution. The growth was remarkable. In 1839, the value added to the American economy equaled $787 million from agriculture and $190 million from manufacturing. By 1859 it equaled $1,492 billion from agriculture and $859 million from manufacturing, a nearly fivefold increase in value added from manufacturing and only a doubling from agriculture (Gallman 1960, Table 3).

The organization of work in the factory differed markedly from the organization of work on the farm or in the household. In the Jeffersonian ideal, the farmer who worked the land was free, and he worked in such a way and for such a purpose as to cultivate virtue. What was important to civic virtue as far as Jefferson was concerned was the independence, the ability of a person to make decisions for themselves. This economic independence, Jefferson felt, breeds political independence on the one hand, but concern for neighbor, community, and country on the other hand. While the hours were equally long, the organization of work in a factory was different in nearly every other way. In a factory, a worker was not free in the same sense: he answered to a boss and was paid a weekly wage. The worker had no investment in either the factory or the finished product. There was no independence, and thus, in the Jeffersonian ideal, no cultivation of civic virtue as such.

This transition in the nation's political economy was a critical turning point in the development of civic capacities and the motivations for civic participation. Sandel's (1996, ch. 6) analysis of the debate over free labor versus wage labor is instructive in understanding this transition. As factory life became an increasingly common component of the American economy, the reality of wage labor rubbed up against the Jeffersonian ideals that political liberty required economic freedom: that economic freedom cultivated a particular kind of civic virtue that America needed to survive. American democracy "demanded independence, not only political but economic; it demanded the maximum diffusion of self-reliant habits . . ."(Rogers 1978, 33).

How, then, did the political philosophy of republicanism respond to the realities of wage labor and an increasingly important industrial economy? After all, it would seem an impossible accommodation to make: economic freedom was political freedom's sustenance. Yet the nation's economy was quickly moving in such a way that made economic freedom for individual people difficult, if not impossible, because they were working for a wage rather than for themselves. As Sandel notes, the answer lies as it often does in the revision of the ideal. Wage labor could be consistent with political freedom as long as the arrangement was a voluntary one, one where the worker and the employer entered into a voluntary agreement (1996, 194).

The shift in the nation's economy from 1789 to the turn of the twentieth century from one dominated by agriculture, trade, and small household manufacturing to one increasingly dominated by industrial manufacturing, dramatically shifted the balance between civic duty and self-interest even further toward self-interest. This shift can be most evidently seen in the way traditional success was defined in America. In early republican political and social culture, success was defined in terms of the competent, independent, honest, hard-working yeoman who might not become wealthy but would serve his family, community, and nation well by living a moral and virtuous life. By the end of the nineteenth century, success was increasingly defined in terms of individual riches gained through competitive success. As Rex Burns argues, "As the century passed . . . the celebration of competition grew frantic . . ." (1976, 51). The shift was increasingly noticeable by the mid-nineteenth century in popular magazines such as the *Companion*, with articles entitled "How to get a Farm," "How to Make Money," and "How to be Rich" (Burns 1976, 61). But, perhaps the dime novels of Horatio Alger, Jr., popular in the late nineteenth and early twentieth century, best exemplify the shifting ideal away from a republican virtue of civic duty toward a virtue of self-interest. Alger's novels had a common theme, which was the rise of the hero, usually a fatherless boy of modest means, from rags to riches due to his hard work, honesty, shrewdness, and bravery. The antagonist was usually a less intelligent and often villainous and cowardly character (Allen 1952, ch. 4). The moral of the Alger novels was that hard work, thrift, and common sense, when put to good competitive use, would lead to individual economic success. It was a moral ripe for the times: perfectly in tune with the idea of economic capitalism. But the civic virtue it taught was dramatically different from the civic virtue of a republican political economy. Fundamental to the political economy of individual capitalism was individual riches, rather than civic duty.

THE RISE OF THE CONSUMER ECONOMY

As destructive to traditional republican civic virtue as industrial manufacturing was, an even more fundamental shift was on the horizon. When, in 1913–1914, Henry Ford reengineered his automobile manufacturing plant and began making the entire car on an assembly line, the way products were made and sold, and ultimately the ability of consumers to afford them, changed forever. While the principle of the assembly line was not new, Ford's application of it was sophisticated and a vast improvement over the work of Eli Whitney, Henry M. Leland, Frederick Winslow Taylor and others (Allen 1952, 111). The assembly line and the mass production of consumer goods that it made possible fed a growing desire on the part of Americans to have more of nearly everything. Indeed, this was Ford's goal. The genius of Ford, as Watts describes it, is an idea seen as common today: lower prices allow for more sales and a wider pool of potential customers, which ultimately creates demand for more products and sales. Ford's objective was to appeal to a mass of new consumers, and he understood consumer behavior as well as anyone ever has, arguing, "[W]e're creating new wants in folks . . . and we no sooner get those wants satisfied in one class of society than another class bobs up to present its needs and demands. The wants keep right on increasing, and the more wants the more business . . .(Watts 2005, 116). The shift to a consumer-oriented economy, which began in the late 1800s and took off in earnest after World War I, fundamentally altered the Jeffersonian notion of civic duty and replaced it with a civic mindset dominated by a virtue of "wants," as Ford would describe them.

It is hard to say what came first, the wants or the availability of things to want. Ford clearly understood that he was creating the want by creating cheap automobiles. In reality,

Ford was simply tapping into a deep cultural vein that had its roots in the London coffeehouses of the seventeenth century. However, a rapid acceleration began in earnest after the Civil War when, William Leach argues, "American capitalism began to produce a distinct culture, unconnected to traditional family or community values, to religion in any conventional sense, or to political democracy" (1993, 3). By the end of World War I this new culture was clear: the road to happiness ran straight through the department store chock full of products people never knew they needed, and the civic virtue of Jeffersonian republicanism was nowhere to be found on the aisles of different varieties of forks, knives and spoons, mixing bowls, artificial jewelry, ready-to-wear clothing, shoes, lamps, rugs, pianos, bicycles, and the like. The department store did not exist prior to the late 1800s. Most people purchased their necessities from local trading stores, shops, dry goods stores, and large wholesalers. The famous department stores of the big cities took shape in the first decade of the new century: Marshall Field's and Carson, Pirie, Scott in Chicago, Macy's, Bloomingdale's, and Siegel-Cooper's in New York, Filene's in Boston, Famous-Barr in St. Louis, Wanamaker's in Philadelphia, and Lazarus' in Cincinnati. At the same time national chain stores began to emerge, starting with Sears, Roebuck and Company in 1906 and F. W. Woolworth in 1912 (Leach 1993, 20–26).

The political economy of consumption that emerged in full force following World War I, and the values and civic virtue it encouraged represented a near total shift away from republican political economy that dominated American political debate for over a century. In republican political economy the cultivation of the virtue of civic duty was paramount. As Sandel notes, the world of work was important because it was in the world of work where "the character of citizens was formed" (1996, 224). Hard work, discipline, and restraint led to good individual character, and good individual character led to good civic character. The political economy of consumption was agnostic at best on the question of civic virtue, and thus was effectively tilted away from a virtue of civic duty and toward a virtue of self-interest.

The writings of Benjamin Franklin and Napoleon Hill best exemplify this shift. The two wrote nearly 180 years apart, Franklin just before the founding of America and Hill just as the culture of consumption was becoming entrenched in America. In his essay "The Way to Wealth" written in 1758, Franklin gives advice to a group of people who are waiting outside a merchant goods store and complaining about tough times and high taxes. Franklin's advice characterizes the virtue of self-restraint, hard work, thrift, and simplicity. He says, for instance, "Laziness travels so slowly, that poverty soon overtakes him," "If you would be wealthy, think of saving as well as getting," "You may think perhaps that a little tea, or a little punch now and then, diet a little more costly, clothes a little finer, and a little entertainment now and then, can be no great Matter; but remember what Poor Richard says, many a little makes a mickle, and farther, beware of little expense; a small leak will sink a great ship," and "buy what though has no need of, and era long thou shalt sell thy necessaries" (Franklin 1987, 1294–1302). Franklin clearly saw little use for spend thrifts and excesses.

Hill's 1937 bestselling book entitled *Think and Grow Rich* was among the first in what has become known as the "personal success" or "get rich" genre of literature. In it, he advises readers that the average person can become rich if they simply believe they can and have the desire to do so. In the Introduction, Hill writes: "Truly, 'thoughts are things,' and powerful things at that, when they are mixed with definiteness of purpose, persistence, and a BURNING DESIRE for their translation into riches, or other material objects." Riding the wave of scientific discovery, Hill claims the book is the result of 25 years of research on more than 500 "distinguished men of great wealth." The book is organized around 13 steps to riches, including DESIRE, AUTO SUGGESTION, IMAGINATION, THE POWER OF SEX TRANSMUTATION, and THE SIXTH SENSE

(1937). Hill clearly understood both the availability and desire for riches and material goods, and believed pursuit of them would make people better.

Franklin and Hill's advice are linked to civic virtue in vastly different ways. Franklin's advice is linked to republican notions of civic virtue through self-sufficiency and restraint, both of which would lead to civic virtue. Franklin could have easily said that one who is a spendthrift is less likely to find himself politically independent. Why? Because spendthriftiness was seen as a vice that would lead to economic dependence rather than a virtue that would lead to economic independence. Economic dependence killed virtue, as Jefferson argued, and political independence required it. For the founders, political independence, which was seen as a fundamental requirement for the survival of the new republic, was built upon economic independence. Hill's advice is linked to a newly developing notion of civic virtue that complimented consumerism by encouraging individuals to fully engage with the free-enterprise system of capitalism. Individual successes in this context were linked to civic virtue in a much different way than Franklin would have perceived them to be. Rather than restraint and frugality playing a central role in independence and civic virtue, achievement-oriented thinking and acting that led individuals to pursue their self-interests was tantamount to performing a civic duty because the national economy was increasingly dependent upon a cycle of consumption.

THE CIVIC VIRTUE OF CONSUMER CHOICE

This shift was made possible by the new Keynesian economic philosophy, which took no position on what kind of citizen the economy should produce. Rather than direct an economy that would produce a particular kind of civic virtue within citizens, as Jeffersonian republicans sought to do, a political economy dominated by Keynesian thought cared little about the particular kind of civic virtue of citizens. Instead, it simply responded to consumer preferences and tried to ensure enough consumer demand to keep the economy strong. Sandel argues that the emergence of Keynesian economic thought marked a major shift in the demise of republicanism in American politics and the rise of contemporary liberalism, where the government took a neutral stance on civic virtue and instead left it to individuals to choose what was best for themselves (1996, 262).

This shift from republicanism to liberalism was seen as an enhancement of American democracy by many because it had as part of its goal a broader definition of equality that included economic equality. It also produced what Cohen called the "consumerized republic," where the citizen performed a civic duty simply by consuming (2003). The idea that economic equality was part and parcel of American democracy was articulated to a mass audience most broadly and generally by President Franklin D. Roosevelt in 1936 in accepting the Democratic Party renomination for president. In his speech, Roosevelt argued that the American Revolution gave people liberty by wiping out political tyranny when it gave the business of government "into the hands of the average man who won the right with his neighbor to make and order his own destiny through his own government." But, Roosevelt contended, since then new economic forces had brought about a condition where political equality alone was not enough to foster liberty; instead, liberty required economic equality as well. "If the average citizen is guaranteed equal opportunity in the polling place," Roosevelt argued, "he must have equal opportunity in the market place [as well]" (Democratic Party, and Oliver A. Quayle 1936).

So, Roosevelt proposed that modern democratic governments had certain obligations to their citizens, including the establishment of a democracy of opportunity. This was no idle contention, and it was a dramatic change in the institution of political economy. In the face of economic depression and recession, and totalitarianism and communism spreading around the globe, Roosevelt saw it as an historic moment. "It is not alone a war against want and destitution and economic demoralization. It is more than that. It is a war for the survival of democracy. We are fighting to save a great and precious form of government for ourselves and for the world" (Democratic Party, and Oliver A. Quayle 1936).

Roosevelt's view about a democracy of opportunity and the role of government in bringing it about were controversial, but a remarkable convergence formed around the new institutional role and importance of mass consumption in stimulating and maintaining economic recovery following World War II. Consumers were seen as the key element in stimulating the economy because as they spent on new products, their spending created demands across the economy. Spending was seen as a civic duty, something good citizens did. Model families were depicted on the pages of glossy magazines sitting around dining room tables in their new homes filled with every imaginable consumer item. Brides were encouraged to buy for their new lives, and in so doing were praised for performing a vital duty in preserving the American way of life. In a statement that would have made Benjamin Franklin wonder if he was in the same country, *Fortune* editor William H. Whyte argued in 1957 that thriftiness was un-American (Cohen 2003, 114–121).

By the 1950s, the American political economy not only actively encouraged self-interested behavior on the part of citizens, but also encouraged citizens to think of their self-interested behavior as fulfilling a greater good. Citizens were encouraged to buy, because buying was good for the nation's economy, and a strong economy translated into a strong nation. Citizens who consumed, the argument went, were thus good citizens who were performing a civic duty, doing their little part to keep the nation strong. The effect on the balance between civic duty and self-interest, however, was to shift dramatically away from the traditional notion of civic duty. Despite the attempted linkage, the idea that self-interested consumption was somehow an act of selfless civic duty simply undermined the value of traditional acts of civic duty.

The notion of consumption as civic duty did not recede as the nation's economy recovered from World War II; rather, it soon became even more important as a central front in a Cold War between the West, but principally America, and the Soviet Union. And the family became a central institutional player. In this new war, guns and tanks were replaced with individual and family-oriented consumer goods. On the home front, Americans were encouraged to continue consuming because the better the quality of life the average American lived, the stronger the ideological argument against communism and the Soviet Union. People around the world were encouraged to compare the standard of living and the consumer items Americans had available to them with those of people living under communist rule. The free market economy and all of its benefits to the average American family was linked without question to political freedom. This linkage was central to the "Kitchen Debate" between Vice President Richard Nixon and Soviet Premier Nikita Khrushchev in June 1957 at the American National Exhibit in Moscow. There, Americans showed off among other things a new color television set, a six-room model home complete with a range, dishwasher, upright refrigerator, and other appliances. Khrushchev also approvingly tasted Pepsi (Hixson 1997, 179–180).

While touring the exhibition, Nixon and Khrushchev began a tense discussion comparing the two societies. Nixon extolled the virtues of the range of choices and opportunities that American consumers had, linking such choices and opportunities directly to political freedoms.

Said Nixon, "To us, diversity, the right to choose, the fact that we have 1,000 builders building 1,000 different houses, is the most important thing. We don't have one decision made at the top by one government official. This is the difference." In other words consumer choice directly equated to democracy.

Khrushchev shot back, "On political problems we will never agree with you. For instance Mikoyan likes very peppery soup. I do not. But this does not mean that we do not get along."

Nixon replied, "You can learn from us and we can learn from you. There must be a free exchange. Let the people choose the kind of house, the kind of soup, the kind of ideas they want."[1]

SELF-INTERESTED CIVIC PARTICIPATION

Nixon's description of the importance of consumer choice in the American political system embodied just how far the civic ideal had shifted since the founding. Nixon's explanation encapsulated how and why the American political economy encouraged civic and political participation. Americans participated by purchasing because purchasing not only kept the economy strong, but helped in the Cold War fight against communism. American consumption represented not only the abundant success of the American economy, but it also represented the political freedoms Americans had, and the extent to which those political freedoms were broadly available across the socio-demographic spectrum. The more Americans who could participate in consumption, the more it represented the successes of the American political system. For Nixon, consumer choice equaled political choice, period.

As Cohen (2003, 127) notes, the logic behind Nixon's explanation became something akin to a national civil religion in the 1950s, a religion that holds a firm grip on the country to this day. What this logic also represents is a solidification of the remarkable shift in the institution of the political economy away from the virtue of civic duty and toward the virtue of self-interest. Remember, civic duty depends on citizens deliberating about the common good and being active participants in shaping the outcomes of those deliberations. Civic duty depends upon citizens keeping up with public affairs and genuinely caring about their communities, and doing those things necessary to ensure the health and welfare of their communities. The consumerized republic encourages citizens to think about themselves, about their wants and needs, their desires, and how to better their individual lives.

While the consumerized republic does not openly discourage civic duty, it actually does something worse than that. By tilting the balance heavily in favor of private good over public good, the consumer republic justifies self-interested behavior *as* civic duty. Just as during the Cold War, one of the central fronts in the war against terrorism was an economic front. Speaking to a joint session of Congress on September 20, 2001, President George W. Bush outlined what he expected of the American people as the country responded to the terrorist attacks nine days earlier. Among the expectations was that Americans would "continue to participate in the economy"; that they would continue to shop. A few days later, during a speech at Chicago's O'Hare airport, Bush urged Americans to "Fly and enjoy America's great destination spots. Get down to Disney World in Florida. Take your families and enjoy life, the way we want it to be enjoyed."[2]

While Roosevelt played a clear role in aiding the development of the consumerized republic, it is interesting to look at what Roosevelt expected of the American people as the country responded to the Japanese attacks on Pearl Harbor and its entry into World War II, and compare those with President Bush's. In his "A Call to Service" speech of April 28, 1942, Roosevelt gave Americans a detailed update on the status of fighting in both the Pacific and European fronts. He then called Americans to service and sacrifice: "[T]here is one front and one battle where everyone in the United States—every man, woman, and child—is in action, and will be privileged to remain in action throughout the war. That front is right here at home, in our daily lives, in our daily tasks . . . Here at home everyone will have the privilege of making whatever self-denial is necessary . . . This will require, of course, the abandonment not only of luxuries but of many other creature comforts." Later in the speech, Roosevelt explained why sacrifice and self-denial were necessary: "The price of civilization must be paid in hard work and sorrow and blood. The price is not too high.

If you doubt it, ask those millions who live today under the tyranny of Hitlerism."[3]

Fifty years later, President Bush's prescription for civic participation in response to the most deadly attack in the nation's history since Pearl Harbor did not call on service or shared sacrifices, but instead called on shopping, traveling, and living life "the way we want it to be." This prescription meant two things. First, it meant that civic participation is easy. If the response to an attack is consuming, traveling and enjoying life, then civic participation is easy, and fun, and people could feel good about doing these things because the president said these were the sorts of things Americans should do as a response to his call to service. In short, civic duty did not have to be anything difficult, or for that matter different from what Americans did day in and day out. It meant that deliberating about the common good, being active participants in shaping the outcomes of those deliberations, keeping up with public affairs, caring about communities, and doing those things necessary to ensure the health and welfare of those communities could all be accomplished by shopping, traveling, and enjoying life.

Second, it meant that civic participation could be carried out in a way best suited to the personal needs and desires of the individual. In a world so full of different consumer goods, different consumer choices, and different consumer opportunities, individuals would have to be selective about which they chose because as much as they might like, they could not choose them all. Thus, inevitably, there could be no shared experience. My particular consumer choice might be totally repugnant to your consumer choice, but that is the glory of America: we are both carrying out our civic duty in making those choices. In America today, consumer choice equals civic duty. The motivation to participate in any form is driven by self-interest.

As an institutional sphere, the political economy is a powerful influence on individuals. But the political economy, like all institutions in society, operates interactively with other institutional spheres rather than independently. As an institution, the political economy in part reflects society's civic mores even as it concomitantly influences them. In this context, as the political economy evolved over the course of two centuries in a way that increasingly encouraged in individuals more self-interested behavior and less civic duty–oriented behavior, the pressures it placed on the institutions of socialization—the institutions that should have in part mediated the deleterious influences of the political economy on those civic mores—was significant, and they bent under the pressure. The family as perhaps the most important institutional repository of much of the civic values and orientations a young person acquires early in life has been embattled for years, but especially in the last half century. For instance, many lament the decline of the traditional nuclear family; declining birthrates, rise of two-worker households, and rising divorce rates, as evidence of the forces lashing at the family. In a chapter in *Bowling Alone* entitled "What Killed Civic Engagement? Summing Up," Putnam notes the changing traditional American family as one part of the explanation: "The downturn in civic engagement coincided with the breakdown of the traditional family unit—mom, dad, and the kids" (2000, 277).

But the traditional family as an institutional sphere is not and has not been alone in its inability to inculcate the civic values of civic duty in the face of a powerful and evolving political economy ceaselessly encouraging self-interested behavior. Schools and the institution of education proved little help to the family, and the media has in many respects joined forces with the evolving political economy to encourage self-interested behavior. As was discussed briefly in the previous chapter and will be discussed more thoroughly in Chapter 5, while there has historically been a struggle in the institution of education as to how best to produce good citizens, the emphasis in civic education given to the image of the self-made man, self-reliant individualism, and benefits of the free enterprise system has played right into the self-interested direction in which the political economy has encouraged Americans. An institutional view that sees

education as a means to economic success, firstly, and producer of good citizens, secondly, works rather well with a
consumption-oriented political economy. And media, especially television, has, since the 1950s increasingly encouraged a self-interested consumer behavior, one that either
simply offers viewers choices or dispenses a kind of Hux-
leyan soma called "cool," as media critic Kalle Lasn argues,
that few can resist (1999).

CONCLUSION

This chapter argues that the political economy of the nation
and the civic-mindedness of its citizens are linked, as Jefferson and other republicans of the eighteenth century argued
they were. As the nation's political economy has evolved
away from its agrarian roots to its modern mass consumption base, the civic-mindedness of its citizens has evolved
away from its heavy edge to civic duty and toward a heavy
lean to self-interest. Jefferson and his fellow republicans
felt strongly that the new nation could not survive as it was
designed to exist unless citizens had a civic orientation and
were committed to their fellow citizens first over their private pursuits. Such a commitment, republicans argued, was
grounded in public virtue, particularly the kind of public
virtue encouraged by an agrarian political economy. Thus,
early American political culture inculcated in citizens a commitment to civic duty, and the nation's political economy
encouraged civic duty over self-interest.

As the nation's political economy evolved, however, the
scales tilted away from civic duty and toward self-interest. As
the manufacturing base of the nation's economy grew and
took hold, more and more people found themselves working for someone else rather than for themselves. The result
was fewer and fewer people free in the Jeffersonian sense of
the term, and thus lacking the public virtue required for a
civic-minded society. The political economy of manufacturing, while not discouraging civic duty, did not favor civic
duty over self-interest. As the nation's political economy

evolved toward consumerism, the scales began to tilt further in favor of private interests. This was first expressed in the pursuit of riches, but eventually the political economy encouraged outright consumption as civic duty. By the end of the Cold War, a generation of Americans had grown up believing that they were serving their country by shopping and consuming.

Thus, in the 200-plus year evolution of the nation's political economy, the scales shifted from promoting civic duty on the part of citizens to promoting a self-interest impulse, and eventually to justifying that self-interest impulse in civic duty terms. The resulting influence on civic and political participation has been deleterious. For many Americans today, the self-interest impulse is the only impulse that drives participation, or the lack of participation.

CHAPTER 4

THE PUBLIC SPHERE,
ACTIVE GOVERNMENT, AND
CIVIC PARTICIPATION

ANDREW JACKSON.

Photo 4.1   Portrait of Andrew Jackson
Andrew Jackson's assertion of executive responsibility for public policy had wide-ranging ramifications for an active national government.
Source: Prints & Photographs Division, Library of Congress, LC-DIG-pga-01161

Photo 4.2   Portrait of Franklin D. Roosevelt
Franklin D. Roosevelt's New Deal programs had widespread popular support.
Source: Prints & Photographs Division, Library of Congress, LC-USZ62-19357

There is a corresponding—even if coincidental—relationship between the size of the public sphere and the activity level of government, and the ability of citizens to participate in civic life. As an idealistic political philosophy, republicanism saw the community as an organic whole, and thus individual members of the community as naturally linked to one another. In this sense, what was important or good for the community was by definition important or good for any individual member of the community. Individual interests were subordinate to the common good, but since the common good was an integration of the entirety of the community, it united all of the individual members of the community in "common feelings founded on common consent" (Marone 1990, 42). It is not that the founders of the United States, who were strong advocates of a republican form of government, were blind to the notion that communities were filled with individuals who might have differing goals and objectives; rather, they regarded these as nonnatural aberrations that were "danger-ous and destructive" and that arose from "false ambition, avarice, and revenge" (Wood 1969, 59).

There were a couple of ways that republican ideals could be corrupted. One was by individuals who were falsely ambi-tious or greedy, which as we saw in Chapter 3 was something many republicans felt a manufacturing and commercial politi-cal economy would encourage, and thus argued strongly for an agrarian-oriented political economy. Another way that republican ideals could be corrupted was by having a public sphere that was too large and would result in too much gov-ernment or a government that was too active. For this reason, republicans argued strongly for a small national government with only limited powers and for most problem solving to be handled at the local level by individual citizens or groups of citizens.

In this chapter I demonstrate that despite these republican ideals, the size of the public sphere and level of activity of the national government began to increase almost immedi-ately. This was the case initially because Presidents Jefferson and Madison used the government in ways that established precedents for an active government, but then over time because people demanded that government do more to solve problems that were too big to be solved by individuals alone. As the national government's role in problem solving expanded it had a correspondingly harmful effect on the cal-culus for civic participation, discouraged participation moti-vated by a sense of civic duty largely by removing the need for it and making it difficult. However, even while this growth in both the size and activity of the national government was taking place, the republican ideal of civic duty persisted (and persists), resulting in something akin to a collective anxiety.

REPUBLICAN IDEALS, THE PUBLIC SPHERE AND THE PROBLEM WITH AN ACTIVE GOVERNMENT

The way the founders saw the role of the individual and the role of government in the public sphere helps explain why they were afraid of too much and too active a government, and sought to have only as much of it as would be needed for protection. Direct citizen participation in civic affairs was the foundational expectation of republicanism—both a right and a duty. That is the only way it could work, and from direct citizen participation natural leaders would emerge to represent the common weal (Marone 1990, 42). A public sphere that was too large and that resulted in too much organized government would take away from both the need for and the ability of citizens to directly participate in public affairs. And, more worrisome, too much government would create conditions for false ambition, avarice, and revenge because it would remove from the community the ability to decide the common good. This was especially true the further removed government was from the people, so too much government at the national level was worse than too much government at the state level, which was worse than too much government at the local level. In a letter to William Johnson in 1823, Thomas Jefferson explains this concern: "I wish . . . to see maintained that wholesome distribution of powers . . . and never to see all offices transferred to Washington where, further withdrawn from the eyes of the people, they may more secretly be bought and sold as at market" (Jefferson 1904, 15: 450).

In general, two important ideological threads survive to this day that have their roots in these early republican ideals: The sense that it is a civic duty for an individual to engage with the public sphere: to participate in community governance and community problem solving (the republican civic duty motivation for participation), and an aversion to too much government or too active a government (linked to the notion that more government equals more corruption). A common explanation for people's involvement in civic and political affairs is a sense of civic duty. Ask most public office holders why they initially ran for office and they are likely to talk about their sense of civic duty to serve. And, while political progressives articulate well the value of active and energetic government in protecting rights and expanding opportunities, they like their conservative counterparts often also decry the corruption found in government.

However, while no founder is more closely associated with republican ideals than Jefferson, the irony is that as president, Jefferson and after him James Madison planted the seeds for what would eventually become an active government much bigger than either one would have imagined, and which would come to occupy more space in the public sphere than either one would have felt comfortable with. In some important ways, republican philosophy did not survive intact its first brush with the practice of governance in America. This irony was first noted by the historian Henry Adams, who chronicled the Jefferson and Madison administrations in his nine-volume history of America from 1801 to 1817. Gary Wills points out that Adam's character sketches of Jefferson show the contradictions in the man that would become the contradictions in the nation: "The federalists were consistent, and imprisoned in their consistency. Jefferson, by contrast, was a localist in theory, the leader of resistance to the Union in 1798, but a cosmopolitan by inclination. Conservative and cramped in his views on what government could do, he was 'prone to innovation' and grand projects that only government could advance" (2005, 137).

Adams describes three areas in particular where Jefferson and Madison laid the foundation for what would become an active government; one that would come to occupy more and more space in the public sphere and coincidentally make the practice of civic duty more difficult. In his inaugural address Jefferson stated his intention to avoid partisanship in office, declaring, "We are all Republicans, we are all Federalists." He called for a wise and frugal government, one that was judicious in the expense of public money and that supported state governments as the most competent administrators of domestic concerns and as the "surest bulwarks against antirepublican tendencies." Yet, as Adams explains, Jefferson very quickly moved to nationalize politics through patronage by firing Federalist office holders and replacing them with Republicans. In defending the firing of Elizur Goodrich as Collector of New Haven, Jefferson had to admit he was engaged in claiming the spoils of victory. He was at the same time laying the groundwork for a federal bureaucracy (Adams 1986a, 152–154).

Republican ideology held militias in high regard and dismissed the need for a standing army. Upon declaration of war with Britain in 1812, Jefferson reassured President Madison that the Virginia militia alone could take Lower Canada—troops from the southern counties could mount a summer invasion and troops from the northern counties could continue in the winter (Wills 2005, 284). However, the American experience at war led Madison to propose the creation of a standing army and navy. In transmitting the treaty ending the war to Congress for its ratification, Madison also called for the permanence of the army and navy. "Experience has taught us that neither the pacific disposition of the American people, or the pacific character of their political institutions, can altogether exempt them from the strife which appears, beyond the ordinary lot of nations, to be incident to the actual period of the world; and the same faithful monitor demonstrates that a certain degree of preparation for war is not only indispensable to avert disasters in the onset, but affords also the best security for the continuance of peace" (Adams, 1986b, 1238–1239). An army and navy, in other words, were needed to back up the nation's foreign policy. Such an understanding of foreign affairs was a far cry from Jefferson's original declaration to avoid "entangling alliances" with other nations.

Finally, having opposed the creation of a national bank and the centralization of finances on ideological grounds in 1791, Jefferson and Madison came to support just such a thing and near the end of his presidency Madison signed the Second Bank of the United States into law. The financial crisis caused by the War of 1812 made the nation aware of the inefficiency of its financial system. Why did Madison change his mind? The state of its finances resulting from the war caused republicans such as Jefferson and Madison to surrender their "cherished constitutional principles and create a 'monster' bank" (Catterall, 1903, 1). Madison defended his switch by essentially arguing that the idea of a national bank had withstood the test of time and had come to be acceptable to the nation at large . . . and that it was "very necessary" (Madison 1865, IV 183–187).

Republicanism as a political philosophy essentially called for a small public sphere with as little government as possible, and for as many decisions as could be made at the local level to be made there. It also called for active and engaged citizens who would put the interests of the community ahead of their own self-interests. Yet, once republicanism triumphed in the second revolution following the election of 1800, Jefferson, and later James Madison, governed somewhat differently. Perhaps it was the inevitable conflict between theory and practice, but the first two philosophically republican presidents planted the seeds for a much expanded public sphere and set in place the foundations for what would become a big active government in America (Ellis 1987, 5). Yet, the philosophy of republicanism did not die; rather, it continues to influence political thought in America to this day, and results in something akin to an internal conflict: at some level we want the active government that we have to solve big and seemingly intractable problems, but at another level we long for the spirit of civic duty and local problem solving that republicanism rooted deeply in our civic hearts.

THE PUBLIC SPHERE AND DEVELOPMENT OF AN ACTIVE GOVERNMENT

One way to describe the expansion of the public sphere and the development of an active government in America is by summarizing the size of government over time in terms of its budgets, number of employees, or departments and agencies. But more fittingly for our purpose would be to summarize the growth of the public sphere: what government has done and how what government has done has increased dramatically over time. What government does, typically, is to solve problems and over time the scope of the problems that the national government has been asked to solve and has attempted to solve has expanded greatly. And as the national government's attempts to solve problems have increased, the ability of citizens to solve those problems has shrunk. From a Jeffersonian-republican perspective, the activities of government, especially at the national level, are correspondingly inversely related to the abilities of citizens to participate, to carry out their civic duties.

While Jefferson and Madison laid the foundations for expansion of the public sphere and a strong and active national government, it was slow in developing. The republican philosophy of localism held a strong grip on the nation during its first century, even among the more "federalist" oriented public officials. Nevertheless, between 1817 when Madison left office and the end of the nineteenth century, two periods of development stand out, both of which involved a concentration of power on the national government. As many scholars of the presidency have pointed out, Andrew Jackson's term in office marked an important turning point in the power of the president, and set the stage for the expansion of executive power. Ironically enough, it was Jackson's agrarian-rooted and Jeffesonian-inspired democratic beliefs that fueled his commitment to localism and states' rights. Yet, it was Jackson's liberal use of the veto in opposing congressional efforts that he felt violated the principle of states' rights and placed too much power in the national government that provided the first glimpse of an active and powerful president.

In the case of his veto of the rechartering of the Second Bank of the United States in 1832, Jackson was making good on his concerns that the bank was a danger to American liberty because it concentrated power in private hands, hands that would inevitably use their power to influence government (Catterall 1903, 247–253; Remini 1967, 44). In this regard, Jackson sounded a lot like Jefferson. Yet in his veto message Jackson argued that the bank was contrary both to sound policy and the nation's welfare (Schlesinger 1945, 43; James 2005, 11–12). The bank veto was only the most important of several in which Jackson took the same approach. His first veto in 1830 was a rejection of a bill to build a road in Kentucky because he believed it was an inappropriate use of federal power for federal money to be used on a local project. He rejected other projects for similar reasons (Ellis 1987, 19–25; James 2005, 11–12). These actions inserted the president into the legislative process and policy making, steps that would empower the executive branch within the national government and empower the national government generally in ways Jackson himself could not only not imagine but would probably find troubling.

The extent to which Jackson's assertion of executive responsibility for policy had wide-ranging ramifications for an active national government became clearer during and just after the Civil War. As Fehrenbacher noted, a disturbing anomaly in American historical literature is to regard Abraham Lincoln as the greatest American president and at the same time recognize that he went further than any other in setting aside constitutional restraints (1987, 113). Citing his constitutional obligations as commander in chief and his duty to faithfully execute laws and preserve, protect and defend the nation, Lincoln blockaded Southern ports, called up states militias, expanded the size of the army and navy, paid soldiers and sailors without a congressional appropriation, and suspended the writ of habeas corpus (Benedict 1991, 46–49; James 2005, 15–16). These actions led contemporary political foes and later historians to call Lincoln a revolutionary in disempowering state governments and centralizing power on the national government (Hesseltine 1963, 36–37).

While both the 1830s and 1860s were periods of greater centralization of power on the presidency and greater centralization of power on the national government, especially in the 1860s, these two periods are better understood as blips. The national government mostly did nothing that had any effect on the day-to-day lives of people. Local governments provided for public safety, education, building roads and streets, public health, and doing what little regulation there was to the economy. The national government kept up a small army and navy, delivered the mail (but only within cities and communities, not across rural America), and paid pensions to Civil War veterans, and to pay for it all it collected small excise taxes and tariffs. Civic participation was an important part of local decision making because the decisions made, such as they related to public safety, education, public health, and the local economy, had an immediate and important effect on the day-to-day lives of people. However, these two periods set the stage for a much wider public sphere and changes in the institution of governance in America in the form of a more active national government, and such a government began to emerge by the 1890s.

EXPANDING THE PUBLIC SPHERE: ACTIVE GOVERNMENT AND REGULATION

The period between the 1880s and 1920s was a transitional period in the American polity (Campbell 1995, 2–4). It is a transition away from the republican era of American politics dominated by an apprehension to centralized political power and toward an era of an expanding public sphere and an increasingly powerful and active national government. Political power was largely decentralized among the various states and the national government, and the republican ideal of individual civic responsibility still had a powerful hold on the country. Americans had always viewed the relationship between liberty and government as a dichotomous one: more of one meant less of the other. This view began to change by the late 1800s, largely because Americans began to see other forces threatening their liberty and thus to ask more of the national government, and in turn to allow it to do more. However, as the national government's role in problem solving grew, the individual's role began to shrink, and along the way the civic duty calculus for participation began to change as well. The national government's role grew in two principal areas that negatively affected the motivation and ability for individual participation: regulation of the economy and commercial activity and the provision of services and the regulation of social life.

The passage of the Interstate Commerce Act (ICA) in 1887 was a landmark piece of federal legislation in that it marked the national government's first tentative steps into regulating the economy and commercial activities across the country. The ICA's target was the railroad industry and the goal was to eliminate discriminatory pricing that hurt small markets, especially farmers in those markets. The act established the Interstate Commerce Commission (ICC) to enforce new regulations. A few years later, Congress passed the Sherman Antitrust Act in 1890, which was designed to ensure that any restraints on trade caused by combination or conspiracy were stopped. In 1914 Congress created the Federal Trade Commission (FTC), which had a broader mandate than its predecessor the ICC. The FTC not only had the legal authority to regulate commerce, but also the responsibility to provide advice, guidance, and information to businesses. Government activities continued and picked up pace across the economy in the decades leading up to the Great Depression (Stone 1991; Keller 1990, 23–33; Campbell 1995, 73).

Thus, within a few short decades the national government went from a largely laissez-faire position regarding the economy and commercial activity to a much more expansive view, and it became much more actively engaged in commercial and economic regulation during this time. Ironically the driving force behind this was the very republican philosophy of localism and the notion that individual entrepreneurship and individual opportunity was being compromised by trusts and large corporations that were not part of the community. Trusts and large corporations were crushing individual entrepreneurship and local commercial activity and they were too large and powerful for local communities or even states to control. The problem was too big for individuals or the community to solve. The national government had to do it. Support for action at a national level was driven by an understanding that the national government, in taking action, was protecting the individual's ability to engage in commerce without being unfairly done in by large corporations and trusts. The public sphere was growing, being expanded by the need to solve problems too big for individuals or communities to solve on their own. The philosophy of republicanism was being turned on its head, shifting problem solving in a big way to the national government.

This shift could be seen in the national government's provision of subsidized services, which benefited mostly rural people at first. For instance, in 1896 the federal government began rural mail delivery for the same cost as mail delivery anywhere. Perhaps the largest and most expensive rural service subsidy came via the United States Department of Agriculture (USDA), which looked after the interests of the largely agrarian population. In 1887 the USDA opened research centers in each state, called Agricultural Experiment Stations, in order to help the agricultural industry solve problems and experiment with new farming and agricultural techniques. By the late 1920s, the USDA was not only a full-blown research and experimentation agency but also a powerful regulatory agency and a provider of direct benefits to farmers and purchasers of agricultural commodities (Wooddy 1934, ch. 12; Campbell 1995, 76–78; Sanders 1999, 391–394).

The increasingly active national government's role in problem solving extended beyond economic regulation and assistance to social regulation and welfare during this time as well. Since the end of the Civil War the federal government had been paying pensions to war veterans. By the 1890s the Pension Office was the largest government office in the world, and by the turn of the century it had paid out nearly $140 million to nearly a million veterans. In 1891 the federal government took over the admission of immigrants from the states and opened Ellis Island the following year. Early immigration restrictions targeted criminals, paupers, the insane, contract laborers, anarchists, prostitutes, and certain national or ethnic groups such as Chinese. The federal government was given explicit authority to regulate personal social behavior with the Eighteenth Amendment to the Constitution in 1891, and quickly criminalized the manufacture and sale of alcoholic beverages (Keller 1994, ch. 6 & 7; Campbell 1995, 78–81).

At the root of this transition was a fear that the republican values of the American political system were being undermined by powerful forces outside of the control of the average American: large manufacturers, central banks and investment houses, railroad barons, forces of immorality and decay, and the like (Wiebe 1967, ch. 3). In response, a multifaceted populist movement sought the national government's help to return American to its past; back to its egalitarian republican principles, public virtue, and industrious communities. Sanders describes the situation in which America's farmers found themselves: "Because they were geographically dispersed and bound up in powerful flows of interstate and foreign commerce, local economic collective action could not provide the alternative for farmers . . . The farmer's enemy was not an employer but a system— a system of credit, supply, transportation, and marketing. To reorder the system required political action at the highest level" (1999, 101). In order to restore and protect the agrarian way of life and economy, oddly enough, a strong national government was needed.

In pursuit of such reform, a diverse group of populist advocates who just as often disagreed with each other argued that the federal government would have to do much more than it ever had to solve these problems and support the common man. Among the proposals were a graduated income tax, government ownership of the railroads, a ban on alien land ownership, shorter work days and better protection of workers in general, prohibition of the manufacture and sale of alcohol, and giving women the right to vote (Kazin 1995, ch. 2). The irony is that the populist movements of the late-eighteenth and early nineteenth centuries, while rooted in a desire for republican principles, encouraged the expansion of the public sphere and an increasingly active national government to solve many of their problems, thus making republicanism in practice more difficult. In many important areas, civic participation toward problem solving became more difficult during this time because problems were and were defined as beyond the scope and ability of individual citizens or communities to solve. In response, citizens looked to the national government for help and the national government increasingly responded. It was a vicious cycle that ultimately contributed to disincentivizing the civic duty motivation for participation.

FURTHER EXPANDING THE PUBLIC SPHERE: THE GREAT DEPRESSION AND DEMAND FOR ACTIVE GOVERNMENT

Having primed the pump, so to speak, for a more active and engaged national government, Americans sought the government's help more than at any other time in the nation's history after the market collapse of 1929. As Walker and Vatter note, "The resultant shock to society and the unprepared government establishment suddenly created thresholds for a number of social and ideological developments that had been brewing for a long time. As the thresholds were reached they surfaced in a surge of societal demands for large government responses. The responses were forth coming" (1997, 29). History often records the Hoover administration as either unresponsive to these demands or resistant to them, but the reality is more complicated. While the public sphere had expanded and the federal government's level of activity and engagement had certainly increased since the end of the Civil War, President Hoover's initial response was informed by the legacy of dual federalism, and the thinking that the national government's role was not to assist the poor, indigent, or unemployed (Shlaes, 2007). These were problems most appropriately handled at the local level by neighbors and communities; by local governments, and perhaps with aid from state governments in a pinch. The federal government's role was coordination and encouragement, not direct assistance, and certainly not programmatic control (Campbell 1995, 84–85).

However, the scope of the economic collapse that began in 1929 caused the Hoover administration to act, even if tentatively. Given President Hoover's adherence to laissez-faire principles and duel federalism, his administration's initial response was designed to assist businesses and not individuals. For instance, the Reconstruction Finance Corporation (RFC), created in January 1932, provided loans to banks, railroads, insurance companies and agricultural corporations, keeping many of these institutions from financial collapse. Although it acted reluctantly, Hoover's moves to shore up the national economy in such a way marked a fundamental shift in the relationship between the government and the private market economy. Both accepted the government's role in helping to soften the impact of a depressed economy on private enterprise (Robertson and Walton 1979, 412; Higgs 1987, 163–165; Walker and Vatter 1997, 34).

But perhaps the most significant element of this shift can be seen in the Emergency Relief and Construction Act (ERCA) created later in 1932. As Studenski and Krooss note, the ERCA marked an even more critical turning point in the relationship between the national government, state and local governments, and the individual by "writing finis to the doctrine that welfare payments to individuals were outside the scope of the Federal government" (1963, 359). The responsibility for problem solving shifted dramatically as a result of the ERCA, which allowed—for the first time— for federal monies to be provided to states for the direct assistance to people in need (Higgs 1987, 164).

What began as hesitant steps by the Hoover administration to expand the public sphere and involve the national government directly in helping the nation survive the Great Depression turned into an outright sprint during the Roosevelt administration. The New Deal, the universal name for the series of programs that the Roosevelt administration initiated to provide relief, recovery, and reform in the wake of the Great Depression, was an extraordinary shift in federal responsibility to the individual, and moved the national government front-and-center into the business of helping individuals solve problems. Several specific programs and initiatives reflected this new view of federal responsibility. The Civilian Conservation Corps (CCC) was created in 1933 in an effort to provide direct relief to the unemployed and others facing financial hardship. Having had some experience putting the unemployed of New York to work on reforestation when he was a governor, Roosevelt envisioned a national effort at conservation by sending hundreds and thousands of jobless men into the forests to work. For the first time in history, the federal government became a mass employer of the unemployed. The Labor Department recruited the men, the War Department ran the work camps, and the Agriculture and Interior Departments organized and supervised the projects. At its height, over 500,000 unmarried men between the ages of 18 and 25 planted trees, made reservoirs and fishponds, built check dams, dug diversion ditches, raised bridges and fire towers, restored historic battlefields and generally improved parks, forests, watersheds, and recreational areas. President Roosevelt considered the CCC one of the New Deal's unquestioned successes (Schlesinger 1959, 336–341).

The success of the CCC at employing the unemployed encouraged Roosevelt, who followed it with the Works Progress Administration (WPA). Created in 1935, the WPA employed nearly 3.5 million people in its first year for wages slightly higher than they would have received on the dole, but not as high as they would receive in the market by a private employer. The WPA projects ranged from building or improving thousands of miles of roads and highways, thousands of bridges, to thousands of public buildings including schools and hospitals all over the country. The WPA workers built nearly a thousand airport landing strips and thousands of playgrounds in communities all over the country. In addition, the WPA's Federal Theatre Project employed people to put on plays and circuses, vaudeville shows, and marionette performances across the nation. The WPA's Federal Writers Project employed thousands of writers to produce publications ranging from state and regional guides to a series on ethnic studies. Similar WPA projects involved the arts and youth (Leuchtenburg 1963, 124–130, Davis 1986, 463–466, Kennedy 1999, 252–254).

But no program more clearly represented the changed assumptions of social responsibility and the federal role in that social responsibility than the Social Security program. Established in 1935, the Social Security Act created a federally administered system of old-age insurance financed by taxes on worker's wages and their employer's payroll. Employees were compelled to participate in Social Security. The Act also established a system of care for the destitute, the unemployed, the crippled and blind, dependent mothers and their children, and for a general public health service (Nash, Pugach and Tomasson 1988, 7–16; Berkowitz 1991, ch. 2). In announcing the program in January 1935, President Roosevelt spoke of his all-encompassing goal for the program. "No one can guarantee this country against the dangers of future depressions, but we can reduce those dangers. We can eliminate many of the factors that cause economic depressions, and we can provide the means of mitigating their results. This plan for economic security is at once a measure of prevention and a method of alleviation" (quoted in Kennedy 1999, 270).

Like many of the reforms brought on by the populist movements of the late nineteenth and early twentieth centuries, the programs of the New Deal had widespread public support. The severity of the Great Depression galvanized mass support for federal action. Millions of people needed help, and while they looked to their neighbors and communities first, and then to their states, little help was forthcoming. The national government was their last best hope, and Roosevelt responded (Walker and Vatter 1997, 47). What made popular support for the New Deal slightly different from the popular support for the populist movements of the late nineteenth and early twentieth centuries is the near total absence of any illusion that the New Deal was rooted in republican principles. While opposition to much of the New Deal could be found in the south, such opposition was rooted in fear of federal power that could be traced to the Civil War. Thus, by the time America entered World War II, the idea that the federal government had an important role to play in helping individual people solve their own individual economic and social problems was an established fact. The public sphere had widened dramatically, and Americans increasingly looked to government to solve problems. The incentive for individual civic participation had shifted.

THE ENTRENCHMENT OF A WIDE PUBLIC SPHERE AND AN ACTIVE GOVERNMENT

At no time in the history of America up to that point had the public sphere been so wide and the national government been as active as it was at the end of World War II. And that level of activity became entrenched in post-war policies in three ways: a more centrally managed economy, increased regulatory oversight, and increased social welfare. Collectively, these activities produced a broad disincentive to civic engagement, and made it more difficult for individuals to participate in decision making in their communities and states.

The Roosevelt administration's response to the Great Depression of the 1930s was to spend money on a host of New Deal programs aimed at relief and recovery. In doing so, Roosevelt was testing—on a wide scale—an economic assumption that increased spending by government during a time of broad economic downturn and would benefit employment and business conditions. The British economist John Maynard Keynes provided a theoretical and conceptual rationale for this activity in his 1936 book *The General Theory of Employment, Interest and Money*. In it, Keynes demonstrated that during times of economic downturn when employment dipped, government could stimulate increased employment either by increasing spending or by cutting taxes. This would inevitably lead to government deficits, but those deficits would be made up when the economy recovered and government could pull back on expenditures or increase taxes. The experience of the Great Depression and the rationale for government actively engaging in economic management provided by Keynes had a profound influence in encouraging a new role for the national government post–World War II as the central economic manager (Ratner, Soltow, and Sylla 1979, 519–520).

The clearest statement of this new thinking, and this new role for the national government came in the form of the Employment Act of 1946. As it was originally proposed in 1945, the legislation entitled to all Americans the opportunity for full-time employment and made the federal government responsible for creating the conditions for full employment by "providing such volume of Federal investment and expenditure as may be needed . . . to assure continuing full employment." The final version of the bill did not contain explicit rights to employment, or make the federal government responsible for maintaining full employment. The final legislation became more a statement of intention rather than a requirement to act (Santoni 1986, 9–12). Nevertheless, as a statement of intention, it was dramatic in that it codified the national government's role in managing the economy. The practical results of this new federal role was the creation of the Council of Economic Advisors and the Joint Economic Committee to help carry out the intentions of the legislation. The national government began taking an active role through fiscal and monetary policies designed to promote managed and stable economic growth, and to smooth out the up and down cycles in the economy.

Closely linked to the national government's more active role in managing the nation's economy was its more active role in regulating many aspects of both public and private life. It is not that the national government did not engage in regulatory activity prior to World War II; it did, but what changed was the scope of the regulation. Prior to World War II, regulation tended to focus on specific segments of the economy such as energy, shipping, or agriculture. Broad and sweeping regulatory legislation seldom got a hearing in Congress and was seldom proposed by the president; however, as Campbell describes it, "A new regulatory impulse, whose common denominator was improvement in the quality of economic activity, burst on the scene in the 1960s" (1995, 127).

We can see this broad and sweeping nature in some of the major federal legislation passed in the 1960s and 1970s. For instance, the Highway Safety Act of 1966 established broad standards for highway safety. The original 13 standards, developed by the secretary of transportation, included guidelines on driver training, vehicle registration and inspection, highway design and maintenance, and methods of traffic control. To help administer the standards, the act created the National Highway Traffic Safety Administration (NHTSA) and the Federal Highway Administration (FHWA). Having entered into the regulation of driving in 1966, it was no stretch for Congress to impose a 55 miles-per-hour speed limit via the Emergency Highway Energy Conservation Act of 1974 in response to the Arab oil embargo of 1973.

Another example of the broad and sweeping nature of the new regulatory impulse was the Consumer Product Safety Act of 1972. Perhaps no piece of federal regulatory legislation better makes the case for the need for national economic regulation than this act. In it, Congress declared that "an unacceptable number of consumer products which present unreasonable risks of injury are distributed in commerce." Congress also declared that the complexity of products made it impossible for consumers to anticipate the risks and that state and local control of consumer products was not adequate.[1]

The post–World War II era also marked the federal government's permanent role in social welfare. The initial federal role in social insurance came via the Social Security Act of 1935, which provided assistance to the aged, unemployment insurance, maternal and child welfare, public health, aid to families with dependent children, benefits for retirees and the unemployed as well as a lump sum death benefit. Social Security survived the end of the Great Depression and

World War II and provided stable ground for the national government to stand on in the 1960s and 1970s when there emerged renewed interest in social welfare. For instance, in 1965 the Social Security Act was amended to include the Medicare and Medicaid programs, which provide health care to the elderly and the poor. A program administered by the Social Security Administration, Supplemental Security Income (SSI), was created in 1974 to provide supplemental income to the aged, disabled, or blind based upon a demonstrated need.

Other federally funded social welfare programs came into creation outside the umbrella of Social Security. For instance, a New Deal-era food stamp program existed from 1939 to 1943 in order to help get surplus food to people who needed it, but could not afford it. The original food stamp program was only temporary, but another pilot food stamp program was authorized by Congress in 1959, and in 1964 President Lyndon Johnson asked Congress to make it permanent, which they did with the Food Stamp Act of 1964. In 1974 the program began operating nationwide. Also, in 1974 Congress created an Earned Income Tax Credit (EITC) as a general tool to fight poverty. The EITC paid cash refunds to qualified people making poverty-level wages who have children. The initial program was modest, but Congress has expanded the credit on a number of occasions since then. Another Depression era program, the Housing Act of 1937, was amended in 1974 to create what became known as Section 8 housing, designed to help people with low incomes afford rents. Recipients of Section 8 housing paid about 30 percent of their income toward rent, and the federal government paid the difference.

By the turn of the century the national government's role in problem solving stretched far and wide. The most active decades were the 1960s and 1970s. During this time Congress passed bills and the president signed them into law that involved the national government in regulating everything from traffic control plans and flammable fabrics to water and air quality. This growth in the activities of the national government was not forced upon the American people nor was it a one-sided partisan affair. The growth in government activity during Roosevelt's New Deal was followed by the Eisenhower administration's acceptance and maintenance of much of the New Deal's legacy. The dramatic growth in government activity in the 1960s caused by Lyndon Johnson's Great Society programs was followed by Richard Nixon who turned out to be nearly as enamored with an active government, creating the Environmental Protection Agency and involving the national government in the first of what would be many social welfare wars: the war on cancer in 1971. And while Ronald Reagan declared that government was not the solution to our problems but was in fact the problem, the size and level of governmental activity did not abate, but grew during the Reagan years and beyond (Kaplan and Cuciti 1986).

A WIDE PUBLIC SPHERE, ACTIVE GOVERNMENT, AND CIVIC PARTICIPATION

Does it matter that the public sphere has expanded dramatically and that the national government has become an active agent in solving the problems of the nation? The question can be both a normative and political one, but for our purposes it is neither normative nor political. It matters only to the extent to which we judge our expectations of civic participation today against the philosophy of republicanism that guided the creation of the nation. The expansion of the public sphere and the national government's active role in problem solving today is in stark contrast to the role that the founders envisioned the national government would play. While Americans may not appreciate the extent to which republicanism represented a fundamental reordering of eighteenth-century social and political life, our twenty-first-century concern about civic participation is in fact a concern about whether the reordering that the American Revolution brought about is still working.

Among the phrases that dominated the revolutionary language of colonial Americans was "public good," and only republicanism, they argued, could guarantee the public good. For the colonists, republicanism did not characterize a particular form of government; rather, it represented the character and spirit of the people. This explains why the founders were able, after a little over a decade of trying, to scrap the form of government created under the Articles of Confederation and institute a new form of government under the Constitution. Their attitude was whatever form of government it would be, it had to allow for and encourage in the people the traits of a sturdy yeoman: frugality, industry, temperance, and simplicity. It had to encourage at a collective level traits that encompassed a scorn of ease, contempt of danger, and love of valor (Wood 1969, 52). In the government, these traits would result in actions designed only for the public good and not for any individual goods. This was, for the founders, the essence of republicanism and so whatever form the government took in a republic, the end should always be for the good of the whole.

In practice, however, the founders believed that the public sphere should be narrow and the national government should be kept small because this would ensure, as much as it would be possible to ensure, that the government acted in the public good. As Jefferson so often argued, the larger the government the more likely there would be corruption, and where there was corruption in government there was by definition the pursuit of individual good over public good. This meant that most problem solving would be best handled by the people suffering the problem or by the government closest to the people most directly suffering the problem. This would make it more likely that individual citizens would be willing to place the public good above their individual desires. Where sacrifice for the public good was needed, individuals had to be willing to sacrifice. Where the community had a problem, individuals had to be willing to give of their time and resources to solve the problem.

The public good depended upon it. The placing of the public good over individual desires is, as we have already noted, the essence of the virtue of civic duty and the virtue of civic duty in practice is civic participation.

As the public sphere expanded and as this expansion became more institutionalized over time, and as the national government grew and came to take on more and more responsibilities for solving problems, the ability and motivation for civic participation changed in two ways. First, over time it has become increasingly more difficult for individuals and communities to meaningfully problem solve on their own. Second, the motivation to participate has changed in part because we have become used to government solving many problems. Problems are likely to be addressed whether an individual or community of individuals participates or not.

American society is so interdependent today and the problems are often so complex that it is difficult to fully understand how to engage, where to engage, or when to engage. Take for example the modern urban metropolitan transportation planning process. If an individual or group of individuals (say, as part of a community association) were to engage in a metropolitan transportation plan update, the level of knowledge required for understanding how and when to participate is enormous. It would require an understanding of the needs and desires of multiple jurisdictions and the state and federal governments, an understanding of the multiple budgets and sources of revenue and the requirements and limitations that come with each of them, and at least a passing appreciation for the complex and complicated engineering involved.

But metropolitan transportation planning is complex and difficult on its face. Let us consider something more local and easier to imagine individual citizens participating in a meaningful way that should not require the same level of knowledge and understanding as a metropolitan transportation plan: local school issues. In response to concerns raised by parents about what their children were eating in the school cafeteria, the school board of a local public school system established a citizen's advisory committee to study the issue and report back with recommendations. A colleague's husband served on the committee and six-months into their study I asked him how their work was going. He was positive about it, but in the process of giving me an upbeat assessment ended up explaining to me how unexpectedly complex the issue was because it involved all sorts of federal and states laws and regulations related to what schools could and could not serve, nutritional content guidelines, how much they could and could not charge, who they could and could not charge, and a myriad of state and federal requirements for making changes to school breakfast and lunch programs. It was not that the federal or state bureaucracy was overbearing, he noted. In fact, his impression was that both the state and federal governments looked favorably upon their work. It was just that the issue of food in the school cafeteria was far more complex an issue than he would have ever imagined it would be.

The motivation for participation has also shifted, but not necessarily because government does not invite participation. Indeed, most activities of government require the solicitation of public input. For instance, the Federal Highway Administration requires Metropolitan Planning Organizations to invite public participation and input. However, given the complexity of many issues and the difficulty with participation related to that complexity, and the fact that something is likely to be done whether citizens participate or not, the incentive to participate is reduced. The fact is, as the public sphere has expanded rather widely, we know that government is working on most problems and it is simply easier in many instances to let it be. It is not quite a free-rider problem, but it is similar. I think of my ability to drive and navigate at the same time as an analogy. Before I got married, I considered myself a rather good driver. I nearly always managed to drive and read road signs at the same time, and seldom got lost. But, one day a few years into married life, as I was trying to navigate rush-hour traffic to get to an event on time, I realized how much I was relying on my wife for navigation. I was constantly asking her what the signs said, where I should turn, how far away the exit was. She certainly had not forced me to rely upon her for help in navigating. It had just evolved that way, and I found it much easier to rely upon her. Over time, my dependence upon her to help me navigate had become institutionalized. Could I do it on my own? Sure, if I had to. But why bother when I know that she will do as good a job and it will make my driving life that much easier.

Finally, couple the expansion in the institution of the public sphere and growth in the size and scope of government, which made civic engagement more difficult, with the evolution of the institutions of citizenship and the political economy, which collectively encouraged a more self-interested kind of participation, and a broader understanding of the institutional influences on individual civic participation begins to emerge. Collectively, the evolution of these three institutional spheres made more difficult and discouraged civic duty-oriented participation and alternatively encouraged and justified as patriotic self-interested participation. Collectively, the evolution of these three institutional spheres altered the delicate balance established by the founders between civic duty and self-interested behavior.

CONCLUSION

This chapter argues that despite the philosophical intentions of the founders in keeping the size of government small and encouraging citizens to engage in problem solving at the local level out of a sense of civic duty, the public sphere began to expand and the level of government engagement in problem solving began to grow almost immediately. Additionally, the expansion of the public sphere and the national government's size and activity level is inversely related to civic participation. The political system created in 1776 was a delicate balance where each part depended upon the other part's health. In order for free people to be able to govern themselves, republicanism required certain characteristics and qualities, and a form of government that would be both dependent upon the civic duty of free people and encourage that civic duty. As the public sphere grew and the national government became more active and engaged in problem solving, especially in solving problems that were more state and local in nature, it had two effects on the motivation for participation. It slowly removed the incentive to engage for the common good by putting the individual good aside in pursuit of the public good. If the national government would solve a problem then it did not require individual citizens devoting time and resources to solve the problem. But more troubling, as the national government assumed more and more responsibility for problem solving, it became increasingly difficult for citizens to engage in traditional civic engagement activities such as individual and community efforts and charities.

CHAPTER 5

CIVIC SOCIALIZATION AND CIVIC PARTICIPATION

The book began with an argument that citizens have from the nation's earliest days been confronted by two different and often contradictory motivations for participation in civic and political life: self-interest and civic duty. While the founders were certainly not of a unified mind on the value of either one to the civic health of the new republic, the civic duty motivation clearly had a powerful hold on the idealistic aspirations of the new nation and its people. Since then, I have argued, the balance has shifted substantially in favor of the self-interest motivation and away from the civic duty motivation. Why is this so? A large part of the reason, I contend, has to do with the historical development of the three large-scale institutions of citizenship, the political economy, public life and the size and scope of the activities of the national government, and how their historical evolution has altered the incentives for participation in such a way as to not only favor but also encourage self-interest over civic duty.

But that is not the whole story. While the historical development of these three large-scale institutions altered the incentives for participation—incentivizing self-interested participation over civic duty–motivated participation—there were also other institutional changes, less historical in nature, which played a role. The rest of the explanation can be found in the important agents of civic socialization, the basic institutions in society that teach civic values and foster civic participation: the family, schools, and media. Verba, Schlozman and Brady (1995) write that depending upon how they are socialized, "individuals stockpile different amounts and different mixes of participatory resources" (1995, 514–515). The amounts and mixes of participatory resources provided by the family, school, and media in recent decades have not been adequate to the challenge presented by the large-scale institutions pushing citizens toward a more self-interested pattern of civic participation.

The complete story, then, is the linkage between the large-scale institutions and the altered incentives for participation brought about by two centuries of evolution in them, and the inability of the important institutions of civic socialization to provide the right mix of participatory resources to endure the trend. While they are always important, in many ways when they were needed in order to counter disturbing trends toward increasingly self-interested participatory behavior among Americans, these institutions of socialization were not up to the challenge. In this chapter I describe the role of the socializing institutions in providing participatory resources to citizens, discuss the important agents of civic socialization and the pressures they have come under in recent decades and how they have socialized in response to those pressures, and finally bring together the various strands of the argument and link the evolution of the large-scale institutions with the weakened socializing institutions.

THE SOCIALIZATION PROCESS AND THE INSTITUTIONS OF CIVIC SOCIALIZATION

Socialization is the process by which individuals in a society learn the formal and informal routines, norms, procedures, and conventions embedded in the organizational structure of society. As an academic topic socialization crosses many disciplinary boundaries, such as sociology, anthropology, psychology, education, and political science. Here we focus on what has traditionally been referred to as political socialization, but what I will call civic socialization. Political socialization was first described by Herbert Hyman (1959) in an extensive review of scholarship on the topic. Hyman defined socialization as learned behavior, as a person learning their orientations early in life as mediated through various agencies of socialization such as family, political parties, and schools. Later definitions of political socialization, such as those by Almond and Coleman (1960), Almond and Verba (1963), Easton and Dennis (1969), and Greenberg (1970) are more restrictive in that they focus the definition more narrowly on the learning of political orientations and political behavior, but Hyman's description is much more appropriate for my frame of reference because it allows me to think through the role of socialization in civic and political participation from a broader civic lens—thus my use of the descriptively broader term "civic" socialization.

Through socialization, citizens learn and what they learn—those formal and informal routines, norms, procedures, and conventions—are important. As Gimpel, Lay and Schuknecht note, while there is certainly no guarantee that what citizens learn will be *healthy* or *good* for the political or social system, there is a normative assumption that what they learn will be supportive of the political and social system (2003, 13). Dennis calls this the "system relevance" question: what effect does socialization have on political and social life, and does it impede its development or encourage its stability? (1968, 89) Easton argues that the goal of socialization is to develop and encourage the stability of the system through what he calls diffuse and generalized support, which is generated by "the positive encouragement of sentiments of legitimacy and compliance, the acceptance of a notion of the existence of a common good transcending the particular good of any particular individual or group, or the kindling of deep feelings of community" (1965a, 125).

By diffuse and generalized support, Easton is referring to support for which citizens require no particular *quid pro quo* because they broadly support the political system and generally accept the way the system operates, even if they are unhappy with any particular outputs of the system or are somehow negatively affected by those outputs. Diffuse support exists simultaneously with specific support, which is support for the system stimulated by the satisfaction of specific demands placed upon the system, or at least the expectation of that satisfaction in the future (Easton 1965b, ch. 17).

Diffuse support is conceptually similar to the civic duty motivation for participation, where widespread citizen participation is the norm *not* because citizens expect anything in particular in return, but because they are committed *writ large* to the health and stability of the political system. This is why, for Thomas Jefferson, George Washington, and other founders the civic duty motivation for participation was so important. Participation caused by a sense of civic duty is an act of diffuse and generalized support for the political system. Specific support is conceptually similar to the self-interest motivation for participation, where participation is motivated by desires to protect interests and advance causes.

In order to fully understand how the historically evolving large-scale institutions of citizenship, political economy, and the public sphere and active government influenced the motivations for participation we must also have some sense of the role of civic socialization, and in particular the way key socializing agents—principally the family, school, and media—were developing themselves between the late 1950s and the mid-1980s. In an ideal situation, the socializing agents would mediate the macro-trends and counter the shifting balance toward the self-interested motivation for participation by elevating the importance of, or at least maintaining the importance of the civic duty motivation. However, the socializing agents were themselves undergoing change during this time that made such mediation difficult.

SOCIAL LEARNING AND CIVIC SOCIALIZATION

As we have noted, civic socialization is important because it is the process by which individuals learn important information about their society, but what specifically do people learn? According to Easton and Hess (1962) they learn orientations—knowledge, attitudes, and standards of evaluation—about the institutions, both major and minor, of society: the people who run these institutions, the rules by which the institutions and people operate, and the expectations of citizens. It is through civic socialization that people learn basic orientations and patterns of behavior about the political process, about the institutions of government, and about other important institutions within society, both political and nonpolitical. This learning results in opinions on specific civic and political issues such as the value of volunteering, the merits or drawbacks of public funding of elections, or the problems with the public education system. It results in attitudes toward and feelings about political and civic authorities, such as the police, teachers, or the clergy. It results in attitudes toward or feelings about rules, such as the importance of obeying the law, or when civil unrest is warranted and when it is not. It results in general ideological orientations, such as liberal, conservative, or libertarian, and political party identification. It results in attitudes toward or feelings about participating in society, such as whether voting is worth it or not, whether elected officials listen, or the value of civic league participation. At an aggregate level, it results in general attitudes toward or feelings about the political system and society as a whole, such as general patriotism or general alienation.

In its totality, people learn from the socialization process the content that they need in order to participate in the civic and political system. This content is important at both an individual and a systemic level. At the individual level, as we have just described, people acquire very basic and practical orientations. At a systemic level, civic socialization helps the civic and political systems cope with both the internal and external stresses and strains they are constantly confronted by. Among those internal stresses and strains a system confronts are constant changes in its economic, cultural, and social institutions (Easton and Hess 1962, 231). Thus, what people learn through the civic socialization process—the content of that learning—are the orientations and patterns of behavior they need to navigate the institutions amidst the constant changes taking place within and between them. If this civic socialization process breaks down, then the citizen's ability to navigate institutions that are changing becomes more difficult.

Bandura's (1977; 1986) groundbreaking work on social learning theory helps us understand how people learn the orientations and patterns of behavior that are the content of civic socialization, and how learning can be influenced by the historical changes taking place in the large-scale institutions within society that have been described in the previous chapters. Social learning is a result of experiences in the social environment. A common way that people learn is by watching others and from such observations developing their own orientations and patterns of behavior. Bandura calls this a vicarious capability, and through this ability to learn by vicarious observation people are able to generate rules for themselves and regulate behavior patterns without having to form them gradually through a process of trial and error (1986, 19). Orientations and behavior are directed at accomplishing goals or meeting standards, and whether or not one accomplishes the goals or meets the standards is based as much upon a self-evaluative reaction as anything else. Orientations and patterns of behavior are regulated (rewarded, ignored, or punished) directly by society at large, vicariously by observing how others are treated for some attitude or behavior, and/or internally by self-evaluation of the attitude or behavior.

One's experiences in the social environment can result in either a direct or indirect socialization learning process, or some combination of both. Dawson, Prewitt and Dawson distinguish direct political socialization, which refers to learning content that is specifically political, from indirect political socialization, which refers to nonpolitical attitudes and orientations that will come to shape political attitudes and orientations at some future time (1977, 95). Direct political socialization involves directly imitating political attitudes and behaviors of others, taking on a particular attitude or behavior because one anticipates occupying a particular role in the future, directly teaching political attitudes and roles such as through high school civics courses, and gaining direct political experience such as by working on a political campaign or for a political cause (1977, 95).

We can think of the indirect socializations as civic in nature, and thus we could call it a process of indirect civic socialization learning. There are three ways in which indirect civic socialization learning can occur. Interpersonal transfer is the process of indirect socialization where one comes already equipped with attitudes and patterns of behavior gained from noncivic or political settings that are simply transferred to civic or political settings (Dawson, Prewitt and Dawson 1977, 99–100). For example, a child who has developed a respectful (or disrespectful) attitude toward figures of authority in school would be able to transfer those attitudes to figures of authority in civic and political settings. Hess and Torney note that the transference of attitudes and patterns of behavior are not the result of direct knowledge but rather the result of established patterns of interaction (1967, 20–21). Respect for rules in one social setting may also be transferred to respect for rules in a civic or political setting; conversely, disrespect for rules in one social setting may also be transferred to disrespect for rules in a civic or political setting.

Apprenticeship is the process of indirect socialization whereby one uses skills or draws upon orientations gained from noncivic or political settings and using those skills or orientations to navigate civic or political settings (Dawson, Prewitt and Dawson 1977, 100–104). People acquire many skills in life, such as the ability to effectively negotiate, to read complicated materials, to interact with diverse populations of people in diverse settings, or to follow rules, that are easily applied to civic or political settings. Additionally, many of the orientations acquired in life are acquired in distinctly noncivic or political settings, but are easily applied to civic or political settings.

Generalization is the process of indirect socialization; whereby one transfers or generalizes from a noncivic or political belief system to a distinctly civic or political belief system (Dawson, Prewitt and Dawson 1977, 104–105). Belief is not necessarily based upon experience, and so the transference or generalization of a belief from a noncivic or political setting to a distinctly civic or political setting is the transference or generalization from a non-experience to an experience. Belief systems are varied and broad, including regional, religious, ideological, world view, or philosophical.

There has evolved a large literature on who we learn from, or what Hyman (1959) called the "agencies of socialization." If socialization is the process by which individuals in a society learn the routines, norms, procedures, and conventions of their society, then the agents of socialization are the individuals, groups, or institutions that affect that learning process. The slowly changing social, economic, and political forces embodied in the macro-institutions of citizenship, political economy, and the public sphere and the active government had, as we have seen, an influence on those norms, traditions, and behavioral expectations of society, and those changes appear not to have been well mediated by the agents of socialization. There are many agents of socialization, such as friends, colleagues, and peers, churches and other religious institutions, the workplace, and major public institutions in society, but three institutions of socialization are particularly important in helping us understand the puzzle of civic participation in modern America: the family, schools, and media.

Family

Among the most influential agents of socialization is the family. In one of the first studies of its kind, Gillespie and

Allport reported on the results of their cross-national study of young people and concluded that "the family is the primary social institution . . ." (1955, 8). Hyman argued that a person's political orientation was essentially the product of socialization within the family (1959, 64). More recently Verba, Schlozman, and Burns have called the family "the universal social institution" (2005, 95). As the preeminent agent of socialization the family is important in providing resources, in transmitting specific party identification and broader political orientations. However, much of this positive socialization is dependent upon the structure of the family, and in the last half century the structure of the American family has changed dramatically.

As a conduit for resources, nothing is as important as the family. Scholars have noted for years the strong positive relationship between socio-economic status—the combination of education, income, and occupation—and civic and political participation (Verba and Nie 1972; Wolfinger and Rosenstone 1980; Rosenstone and Hansen 1993). For instance, Plutzer (2002) shows that higher socio-economic status parents pass on advantages—namely education—to their children, which lead in part to their children voting at higher rates than children of parents who are not able to pass on similar advantages. According to Verba, Schlozman, and Burns, coming from an economically advantaged family setting is broadly civically enabling; that is, children raised in families with higher socio-economic status end up having greater access to education and better jobs which leads to the acquisition of better civic skills, and ultimately places them in a higher socio-economic position that in turn is linked to networks through which recruitment into civic and political activity takes place. The key vehicle of transmission of civic and political activity is education. Well educated parents produce well educated children, who are enabled to take advantage of all the factors that lead to greater levels of participation (2005, 98).

The family is also important in transmitting partisan identification. Jennings and Niemi (1974) and Tedin (1974) found a strong relationship between parent's party identification and child's party identification. Partisanship is unlike most other political characteristics in that it is for the most part a permanent and salient generalized posture toward the world. This makes it much more likely that children will be able to pick up their parent's partisan orientation regardless of whether the parent intentionally tries to expose it or not. Indeed, Jennings and Niemi conclude that "it is not much of an exaggeration to say that parents socialize their children despite themselves" (1974, 61). It is also clear, however, that children have an easier time picking up on the partisan and policy orientations of their parents when partisan issues are more prominent. The prominence of partisan issues makes the child's job of detecting their parent's orientation somewhat easier (Tedin 1974). Children learn party identification early as well, and what they learn has a lasting influence. Greenstein found that children become attached to a political party long before they know anything substantive about the political parties and their differences (1965, 21), and Abramson showed that once formed, partisan identification is relatively stable and not easily changed (1983).

While agreement between parent and child on partisan identification is strong, research suggests that such agreement on more general political issues requires certain conditions. Dawson, Prewitt, and Dawson concluded that where parental articulation of general social and political orientations was lacking, other socializing agents (such as schools and peers) were more influential. But, when parental articulation was present, it was most influential (1977, 134). For instance, Jennings and Niemi found political issues that struck deep-seated emotions and that were highly salient in the population (such as gun control or school prayer) were more likely to be issues where parent-child agreement was strongest because, in part, those issues were salient to both parents and children. Most issues, they conclude, are too remote from the everyday concerns of people to have a similar level of agreement (1974, 78–81). Tedin also demonstrated that transmission of political orientations was stronger when an issue was salient and the child was able to detect the orientation of the parent toward the issue (1974).

Thus, we see that the family plays an important positive role in the socialization process, but this positive role is associated with two-parent homes. For instance, on almost every indicator of general orientation in Jennings and Niemi's study—political knowledge, cosmopolitanism, political trust, political efficacy, and good citizen attributes—the effects of two-parents was greater than the effects of one-parent only on parent-student similarity (1974, 155). Students who come from two-parent homes are more effectively socialized by those two parents than are students who come from one-parent homes by their one parent—usually the mother.

Family structure is also related more broadly to self-efficacy and self-esteem. For instance, Yabiku, Axinn, and Thornton show that the higher the level of family integration and social interaction, the higher the level of a child's self-esteem (1999). Children from single-parent homes are also less likely to have levels of self-efficacy as high as those from two-parent homes (Gecas 1989). In one of the most comprehensive comparisons of the differences in political socialization outcomes by whether a child's parents were single or married, Gimpel, Lay, and Schuknecht report striking differences. In all racial and ethnic groups except Latinos, across most measures of socialization, children from two-parent homes ranked higher than children from single-parent homes. The one category where youth from single-parent homes ranked higher was on negativity toward policy and courts (2003, 77).

If the family as an institution plays an important positive role in the socialization process, and if this positive role is associated with two-parent homes, then the trend presented in Figure 5.1 is troubling. In 1960 less than 10 percent of children lived in a home with only one parent, but that percentage rose steadily through the decades of the 1960s, 1970s, 1980s, and into the mid-1990s, leveling out in 1995 at around 28 percent, where it has remained. In real terms, more and more children are growing up in single-parent households, and the research suggests that

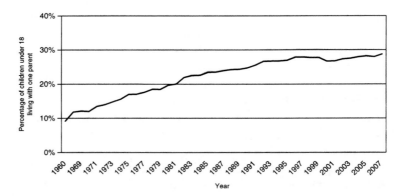

Figure 5.1   Childhood Living Arrangements, 1960–2007

Source: U.S. Census Bureau, Current Population Survey, March and Annual Social and Economic Supplements, 2007 and earlier.

Source of 1960 data: U.S. Bureau of the Census, 1960 Census of Population, PC(2)-4B, "Persons by Family Characteristics," tables 1 and 19.

they are not benefiting from the positive civic and political socialization that comes from two-parent households and are thus less likely to learn the customs, norms, traditions, and behavioral expectations of their society. Without proper mediation from parental socialization, the slowly changing social, economic, and political forces embodied in the macro-institutions of citizenship, political economy, and the public sphere and active government have a much more powerful influence on the customs, norms, traditions, and behavioral expectations that children learn as they grow. In short, as the macro-institutions evolved to incentivize and encourage self-interested behavior more and more and civic duty–motivated behavior less and less, the family as the most important institution of civic socialization was increasingly unable to stand in the gap and mediate the effects on young people.

Schools

As an institution of civic socialization, the school is important in providing knowledge about the civic and political system, instilling loyalty to the country, encouraging compliance with rules, and instilling general support for democracy. The nineteenth century education reformer Horace Mann argued that there was an important role for the schools in instructing a public morality in children in order to prepare them for the responsibilities of citizenship. In his "Report of 1845" as Secretary of the Massachusetts Board of Education, Mann posed a rhetorical question: would the public schools "cultivate the higher faculties in the nature of childhood—its conscience, its benevolence, a reverence for whatever is true and sacred . . ." or the lower instincts and selfish tendencies in people (1868, 421)? He argued for the former, that schools had a responsibility for civic and political socialization. "In order that men may be prepared for self-government, their apprenticeship must commence in childhood. The great moral attribute of self-government cannot be born and matured in a day; and if school children are not trained to it, we only prepare ourselves for disappointment if we expect it from grown men" (1868, 455).

Mann's view of the role of schools in inculcating civic and political values and norms has had a strong hold on American political and educational thought, best exemplified over time in the writings of John Dewey ([1916] 1966) and Charles Merriam (1931; 1934). In their landmark study on the development of political attitudes in children, Hess and Torney find that "teachers transmit a large share of information about the governmental system . . . they are held responsible for presenting material about the government's organization and operation and for inculcating norms of citizen behavior" (1967, 13). Dawson, Prewitt and Dawson note that schooling helps children acquire the cultural norms and expectations associated with membership, and among the methods used is formal instruction in civics and government "designed to acquaint the adolescent citizen with the nature and glory of the established order" (1977, 140).

Among the most important resources schooling provides is basic knowledge about the civic and political system. While civic and political learning certainly takes place outside of the formal classroom setting (such as at home, on the playground, and in popular culture), a solid body of evidence shows that formal education is one of the most consistent contributors of basic and advanced political knowledge (see for example Hyman, Wright, and Reed 1975; Delli Carpini and Keeter 1996; Nie et al. 1996; and Niemi and Junn 1998). Niemi and Junn studied the effects of schools and civic curricula in relation to other factors that lead to civic knowledge and found formal education to be among the most important contributors of political knowledge: "Civic knowledge clearly has many sources, of which the civics curriculum is among the most important; it remains significant and of substantial magnitude against some tough competitors" (1998, 149).

Schooling is also associated with instilling patriotism and loyalty to the country, encouraging compliance with rules, and instilling general support for democracy. In what Dawson, Prewitt, and Dawson (1977, 146) refer to as "classroom ritual life," patriotism and loyalty to the country are encouraged. Rituals such as singing the national anthem, honoring national heroes and events, and hanging pictures and photos of national leaders stresses the importance of loyalty as a function of citizenship to students. In addition, Hess and Torney report that a major emphasis of civic education in elementary school is focused on compliance with rules and to authority. Much of what is called citizenship training in early schooling is focused on teaching respect for the rules and standards of conduct. (1967, 217–218). Finally, Dawson, Prewitt, and Dawson note that teachers are the primary disseminator of values commonly shared within society, such as faith in the American form of government or general support for democratic practices and democratic values (1977, 150).

If the school is important in providing knowledge about the civic and political system, instilling loyalty to the country, encouraging compliance with rules, and instilling general support for democracy, then the changes in civics education that took place in the 1960s and 1970s are instructive and important in helping us understand why the school as an agent of socialization has had trouble mediating the influences of institutional change. As Niemi and Hepburn (1995) note, the curriculum for civics and government classes in the United States prior to the early 1970s focused on how the political system functioned (such as how the three branches of government interacted with each other or how a bill became a law), the obligations and responsibilities of good citizenship, and upon the free enterprise system. In his early 1960s content analysis of civic education texts from three Boston area high schools, Litt found that references to the democratic creed far exceeded any other references (1963, 71–71). Such references had been common in high school government and civics textbooks for decades. For instance, the Virginia edition of the 1923 textbook *Elementary Community Civics* states "a citizen has duties toward his government. If he is protected by it, he must give it support . . . If his government gives him the privilege of voting for officers, it is his duty to accept the privilege and make us of it" (Hughes 1923, 29). The 1948 textbook, *American Government*, equates good citizenship with good sportsmanship, arguing, "If a democracy is to be a success, its citizens must have a sense of good sportsmanship. This means that they should be good losers and generous winners" (Magruder 1948, 636). A commonly used 1950s textbook, *Civics for Americans*, states bluntly the expectations of good citizenship: "Whatever their reason, if it is physically possible for them to get to the polls, and they do not take the trouble to go, they are poor citizens. For voting is not only a privilege. It is also a duty in a self-governing nation" (Clark, Edmonson, and Dondineau 1954, 315).

What replaced this "classic" and civic-duty oriented curriculum? Beginning in the 1970s civics and American government textbooks began to focus attention on political behavior, comparative politics, and quantitative analysis over the structure and function of government, and the obligations of citizenship. In the 1990s, civics and American government courses (as with many other subjects in junior high and high school) became increasingly linked with television viewing, with many schools adding lessons on current affairs and media content from sources such as Channel One and The CNN Newsroom (Niemi and Hepburn 1995). These changes resulted in much less focus on civic socialization and the expectations of good citizenship. These changes were also accompanied by an increasing focus—as seen in the No Child Left Behind program of the Bush era and the continued focus on college and career-ready skills of the Obama era—on the school as a place to learn measurable skills that will be marketable in the economy and give students easier access to economic opportunity.

What Americans have come to expect from schools reflect these changes. For instance, in their study of social studies teachers in America, Farkas and Duffett (2010) note that the last time questions related to citizenship were asked in the nationally representative Phi Delta Kappan/Gallup Poll in 2000, respondents reported that the least important purpose of schooling was to "prepare people to become responsible citizens." More important were things such as "enhance[ing] people's happiness and enrich[ing] their lives" and "dispel[ling] inequalities in education among certain schools and certain groups." In the forward to the Farkus and Duffett (2010) study, Hess and his colleagues lament the fact that education is seen today more as a path to personal and professional advancement than a place where citizenship socialization takes place: "When citizenship is spoken of today, it is often in a 'transactional' sense—with citizenship understood as the basket of skills and attitudes (how to shake hands, speak properly, and be punctual) that will help students attend prestigious colleges and obtain desirable jobs" (2010, 3).

While it is clear that the civics and government curriculum began to change in the 1970s, the point here is not that the changed curricula is problematic *per se*, but rather that the curricula change increasingly encourages a self-interested orientation in students rather than a civic-duty orientation in them. Additionally, the changing curriculum and its changing motivational orientation occurred precisely at a time when Americans, and especially young Americans, were responding to the convergence of the social, economic, and political forces embodied in the macro-institutions of citizenship, political economy, and the public sphere and active government. The old curricula focus on institutions and citizen obligations focused on rules and norms that provided knowledge about the civic and political system, instilled loyalty to the country, encouraged compliance with rules, and instilled general support for democracy, collectively a civic-duty orientation. In the context of the institutional changes described in this book, the new curricular shifted away from the civic-duty orientation. It focused on political behavior, comparative politics, quantitative analysis, and education as a path to personal achievement and shifted the rules and norms, undercutting the stability of the old rules and norms just when they may have been needed the most.

Media

As a socializing institution, the media is increasingly important in providing information, but that information may not be as good for traditional civic and political participation as it once was, and much of that information increasingly encourages self-interested consumerism rather than civic-mindedness. There is a general agreement among scholars that increased exposure to media lead to increased knowledge about civic and political issues and the civic-political process (Chafee et al. 1970; Atkins and Gantz 1978; Garramone and Atkin 1986). Chaffee et al. (1970) report that mass media is the single most important source of political information for children. Garramone and Atkin (1986) show that exposure to both broadcast and print media are related to increases in civic and political knowledge, although exposure to broadcast media is more strongly related to current events' knowledge than is exposure to print media. However, levels of civic and political knowledge have not kept up with the rapid increase in the amount of mass media outlets, suggesting that there is a leveling off point at which increased exposure no longer corresponds with increased knowledge (Zukin 2000).

What specifically civic and political affairs are children knowledgeable about because of their exposure to the media? Increasingly it would appear as though they are knowledgeable about scandal and corruption. As Gimpel, Lay, and Schuknecht note, because people pay more attention to negative or bad news, the media has an incentive to cover negative or bad things (2003, 35), and this incentive is heightened in an increasingly competitive media environment with more and more media outlets competing for the attention of viewers. Additionally, the media is increasingly becoming a part of the coverage of negative and bad things. Sabato contends that an increasingly common spectacle in American public life is the news media going after a wounded politician and in the process the journalists covering the story "take center stage . . . creating the news as much as reporting it . . ." (1993, 1). This approach is also the central critique of the media leveled by Fallows (1996), who argues that the media's method of coverage (journalists participating in talk-show yelling matches instead of simply reporting the news, going on the speaking circuit for large fees, and becoming a part of the story rather than simply reporting the story) is contributing to the increasingly cynical attitude citizens have toward politics, politicians, and public life.

The media also plays an important role in encouraging self-interested consumption. As was described in Chapter 3, the political economy has evolved in the last 235 years from a largely agrarian and trade-oriented one that encouraged communitarian-oriented civic virtue to a consumer-oriented one that encourages a self-interested consumer-oriented virtue. Central to the consumer-oriented economy is the media, and much of what Americans have been exposed to in the media over the last half century has encouraged self-interested consumption, even turning self-interested consumption into seemingly virtuous causes at times. Advertising in all forms, but especially on television, has been the primary driver of this self-interested consumption, and the level of advertising since the 1950s has increased dramatically. Frank (1997) notes that in the six largest media markets, advertising expenditures went from around $4 billion in the mid-1950s to over $12 billion by 1970. By the early 1990s, the average American saw over 20,000 television commercials in a year and in the course of a lifetime would be subjected to over a million advertising "exposures" in forms such as junk mail, billboards, magazines, newspapers, radio, and television. As Kline blithely notes, "We live in an era when it seems obvious we should always be thinking about goods" (1993, 10–11).

While media advertising is directed at all segments of the population, in the context of our present study one segment of the population that is of particular interest is the adolescent population. As Kapur notes, since the 1950s the media has transformed the twentieth-century notion of children as "innocents in need of protection to one of children as sovereign, playful, thinking consumers. Children—that is, preteens—have emerged as the fastest growing market segment based on the premise that the earlier they are hooked on brand names, the longer they will stay with a particular product" (1999, 125). And just what are the socializing effects of all of this media advertising on American children? According to Seiter (1993), happiness and success, in one form or another, has been a central theme of advertising to children, but the effects of this do not lead to increased civic-mindedness. Berman's critique of the culture of consumerism's influence on children is stinging, but probably close to the mark: "Disney, now linked to McDonald's in a cross-licensing partnership, organizes play around its own version of American values, giving our children toys, dolls, coloring books, and images that are burned into their brains . . . our entire consciousness, our intellectual-mental life, is being Starbuckized, condensed into a prefabricated designer look . . ." (2000, 130).

The point of this is not to condemn the media writ large, but rather to demonstrate it as an institution that conveys important (and the importance of) information to citizens about civic and political matters, the media has increasingly come to play a less constructive role just as society has needed it to play a more constructive role. Just as the slowly changing social, economic, and political forces embodied in the macro-institutions of citizenship, political economy, and the public sphere and active government converged in time to incentivize and encourage self-interested behavior more and civic duty–motivated behavior less and less, the media itself was evolving in two ways, neither of which served to mediate the macro-trends. The first was a role that involved greater coverage of scandal and corruption and the second was a role that involved the encouragement of selfish consumerism. Combined, the media encourages greater cynicism and skepticism in public affairs and encourages more self-interested behavior.

CIVIC SOCIALIZATION, INSTITUTIONAL EVOLUTION, AND THE MOTIVATION FOR PARTICIPATION

As institutions of civic socialization, the family, school, and media are the primary ways in which people learn the formal and informal routines, norms, procedures, and conventions embedded in the organizational structures of society. These institutions of socialization have a real and weighty influence on the civic and political behavior of individual people, and as this chapter has shown, these institutions have over the last half century gone through changes that hindered their ability to mediate the slowly changing social, economic, and political forces embodied in the macro institutions of citizenship, political economy, and the public sphere and active government, which were increasingly encouraging self-interested behavior and discouraging civic-duty motivated behavior.

The positive socializing benefits provided by a two-parent family, namely the provision of resources and the transmission of partisan identification and broader political orientations, have been undercut to some extent by the drop in the number of two-parent families since the early 1960s. Since 1980, over 20 percent of all children have grown up in single-parent homes. Such change has no doubt had an influence upon the ability of the family as a socializing institution to effectively teach the routines, norms, procedures, and conventions supportive of traditional forms of civic and political participation.

The resources supportive of traditional civic and political participation provided by the school, namely knowledge about the civic and political system, the instillation of loyalty to country and support for democracy, and the encouragement of compliance with rules, have been undercut to some extent by the changed curriculum since the 1970s. Lamenting this change, one scholar complained, "The public school system has virtually ceased to engage in the kind of civics education that many older members of the discipline [of political science] remember" (Bennett 1997, 50). Civics education since the 1970s has focused more on the behavior of individuals and analysis of data as opposed to the structure and function of institutions and the responsibilities of citizens in the context of those structures and functions. The result of this institutional reorientation has been a behavioral reorientation away from the duties and responsibilities of citizenship. In addition, the focus of public education in general has shifted to focusing on preparation for personal and economic achievement to some extent at the expense of citizenship education.

Finally, the resources provide by the media, namely civic and political knowledge has changed dramatically in recent decades, and the change has meant that the media has come to play a less constructive role in support of traditional civic and political participation and increasingly encourages self-interested consumptive behavior instead.

The media's increased focus on scandal and corruption, and the increasing participation of journalists in news making, has undercut the media's role in providing important information about the routines, norms, procedures, and conventions supportive of traditional forms of civic and political participation. Instead, the media is increasingly the provider of information that leads to cynicism toward and distrust about the civic and political system. In addition, the media increasingly encourages a culture of consumerism where self-interested behavior is predominant.

The changes these institutions of socialization went through, starting in the 1950s and 1960s and accelerating into the 1970s and 1980s, profoundly affected their ability to mediate the shifting incentives for participation that were increasingly discouraging participation for reasons of civic duty while encouraging it for reasons of self-interest. The rules, norms, procedures, and conventions conveyed by the institutions of socialization that would normally mediate the historical-institutional changes by continuing to socialize citizens about the importance of civic duty were unable to do so. Of course, as we know socialization primarily takes place early in life and so we would not expect to see the negative effects on motivation and incentives of the breakdown in the institutions of socialization across all generations equally; rather, we would expect those socialized since the 1970s and 1980s to be more likely to differ in their motivations for participation than those socialized prior to the 1970s and 1980s.

In their study of the four distinct age cohorts that constitute the American population at the start of the twenty-first century, Zukin et al. (2006, ch. 3) demonstrate differences in engagement across generations, especially in what they call electoral engagement and cognitive engagement. When it comes to political activities such as registering to vote, displaying campaign buttons or stickers, or volunteering for a political group, members of the youngest generations (DotNet and GenX) are much less likely to engage in these activities than are members of the oldest generations

(Boomers and Dutifuls). Likewise when it comes to cognitive engagement, a precursor to broader participation in public life, younger generations lag far behind their elders. Members of the Baby Boom and Dutiful generations are more likely to follow government and public affairs, read newspapers and watch television news, and are also far more knowledgeable of current events than are members of the DotNet or GenX generations.

A major study commissioned by the National Association of Secretaries of States (NASS) in 1998 entitled the "New Millennium Project" sought to better understand the problem of declining youth engagement in the political process. The study involved a telephone survey of 1,005 youth aged 15–24 and six focus groups with youth aged 18–24. The report concluded that as institutions of socialization, the family and the schools were failing to adequately socialize youth to participate in the political process. What did young adults say about themselves? The report shows them to be highly individualistically oriented, placing personal goals and success much higher on a priority list than caring about the good of the country or being involved in the democratic process. Only 25 percent gave community involvement a "most important" rating. The report noted that "American youth are not interested in the abstract idea of voting because it's a civic duty, but do respond to the idea of participating when voting will actually affect them" (NEGP Monthly 2000).[1]

The tone of the "New Millennium Project" findings is consistent with results from other recent studies. A 2002 Gannett News Service "Mood of America" poll found nearly six in ten (59 percent) young adults aged 18–30 describing voting as a choice rather than a duty. In contrast, just over six-in-ten (62 percent) older adults described voting as a duty.[2] A 2002 National Civic Engagement Survey funded by The Pew Charitable Trusts found similar differences in motivations for participation between young adults and older adults. Respondents were asked whether being a good citizen meant having some special obligations

Table 5.1   Being a Good Citizen Means . . .

"Please tell me which you agree with more, even if neither is exactly how you feel: Being a good citizen means having some special obligations, or simply being a good person is enough to make someone a good citizen"

Respondents age 15–25:
38.6%—Being a good citizen means having some special obligations
57.4%—Simply being a good person is enough to make someone a
        good citizen
 2.5%—Depends/Both/Neither
 1.6%—Don't Know

Respondents age 26 and older:
47.8%—Being a good citizen means having some special obligations
48.2%—Simply being a good person is enough to make someone a
        good citizen
 1.8%—Depends/Both/Neither
 1.8%—Don't Know

Source: 2002 National Civic Engagement Survey at http://www.civicyouth.org/research/products/data.htm.

or whether being a good person was enough to be a good citizen. As Table 5.1 shows, younger adults have a far different view than do their elders. Nearly six in ten younger adults think being a good person is enough to make a good citizen and only four-in-ten think there are special obligations to being a good citizen. By contrast, older people are evenly divided on the issue.

In Chapter 1 we briefly discussed the findings of a 2006 Civic Health of the Nation Survey that found a majority of Americans saying it was a choice rather than a responsibility to get involved. When we separate the young from the old on this question, we find an even wider gap among the younger respondents and a slight narrowing of the gap among the older respondents. As Table 5.2 shows, nearly six-in-ten young adults think it is a choice to get involved while just about half of the older adults think it is a choice. When it comes to trusting the motivations of others, another question from the 2006 Civic Health of the Nation

Table 5.2 Differing Motivations for Participation by Age Group

"Which statement do you agree with more?"

Respondents age 15–25:
38.5%—It is my RESPONSIBILITY to get involved to make things better for society
57.4%—It is my CHOICE to get involved to make things better for society
2.5%—Depends/Both/Neither
1.5%—Don't Know

Respondents age 26 and older:
41.1%—It is my RESPONSIBILITY to get involved to make things better for society
51.4%—It is my CHOICE to get involved to make things better for society
5.0%—Depends/Both/Neither
2.3%—Don't Know

"Now I'm going to read you some pairs of statements to see how you feel about some matters. Please tell me which you agree with more, even if neither is exactly how you feel."

Respondents age 15–25:
33.9%—Most of the time people try to be helpful
62.4%—Most of the time people are just looking out for themselves
2.6%—Depends/Both/Neither
1.0%—Don't know

Respondents age 26 and older:
41.8%—Most of the time people try to be helpful
51.3%—Most of the time people are just looking out for themselves
4.5%—Depends/Both/Neither
2.0%—Don't know

Source: The 2006 Civic and Political Health of the Nation Survey at http://www.pewtrusts.org/our_work_report_detail.aspx?id=19762.

Survey that we looked at in Chapter 1, young adults have strikingly different views from older people. As Table 5.2 shows, two-thirds of young adults think people are looking out for themselves most of the time while only half of older people feel similarly.

Finally, in Chapter 1 we also briefly discussed a 2010 nationally representative survey of Americans' awareness and understanding of American Constitution, and constitutional concepts commissioned by the Center for the Constitution at James Madison's Montpelier. This study found similar generational differences. When asked to list which one reason from a list of reasons that best described why they would vote in a federal election, only 13.8 percent of respondents between the ages of 18–24 answered "because it is my civic duty", a full 34 percent below the next lowest answer for that category. Nearly a quarter of the 18–24 year old respondents said "To express my opposition to a candidate or issue." The youngest respondents were also far more likely (by 16.6%) than the oldest respondents to agree that a person could still be considered a good citizen even if they chose not to vote.[3]

Taken together, these studies provide convincing empirical evidence of very real generational differences in the motivations for participation, and these generational differences reflect what we would expect to see in the context of the changes in socialization experienced by younger adults as compared to their elders. While we certainly see the self-interest motivation across all generations, younger adults are far less motivated by civic duty and far more motivated by self-interest than are older adults.

CONCLUSION

Civic socialization is the process of learning the formal and informal routines, norms, procedures, and conventions of a society. At an aggregate level, socialization is supposed to keep the civic and political system stable. One of the things people learn from the socialization process is the content that they need in order to participate in the civic and political process. That content—orientations and patterns of behavior related to the political process and important institutions within society—contributes to both the quantity and quality of civic participation. The agents of socialization are the individuals, groups, and institutions within society that affect the learning process: the agents of socialization are the teachers of civic socialization.

This chapter has shown that three of the most important institutions of socialization, the family, school, and media, have undergone changes since the 1950s that have negatively affected their socializing capabilities. These changes—the drop in two-parent families, a shift in the pedagogical focus of civic and political education in high schools, and a media less focused on providing knowledge about and support for civic and political participation and instead more focused on information that lends itself to civic and political cynicism and encouraging consumption—have meant that these agents of socialization have been less able to act as countervailing forces against the historically evolved institutions pushing citizens in a self-interested direction, and that self-interest is clearly evidence in the motivations for participation.

CHAPTER 6

INNOVATIVE CIVIC PARTICIPATION
FOR THE TWENTY-FIRST CENTURY

In this book I have argued that history and institutions matter when it comes to understanding civic participation in America. In focusing on that history and on those institutions, I have asked how they have affected the motivations for individual civic participation. The focus of the book has been on the big picture: the forest instead of the trees. It is not enough to understand that 42 percent of women volunteer for a not-for-profit organization at any one point in time, or that such a percentage of volunteering on the part of women is strongly predicted by their level of education or their income. As important as that information is, the larger context—the historical and institutional forces shaping that behavior—needs to be examined as well. No convincing understanding of the causes of civic participation in America can ignore the influence that history and institutions have on that behavior, and far too often that is precisely what is done.

I began this book by framing our understanding of civic participation, precisely the way many of the founders did: as a human behavior that is driven by motivations, and that those motivations are fashioned (encouraged or discouraged) by institutions within society. The founders understood that institutions within society would have a powerful influence upon people's motivations to participate in the civic life of the new nation; they disagreed about how the institutions should be structured to shape individual and societal motivations. One group argued that institutions should motivate a self-interested behavior because a collective of successful individuals would result in a successful whole. Civic pride, this group argued, would result from success and the power that success brings. The nation would prosper politically, economically, and socially, to the degree to which individuals in the nation were able to prosper. Another group argued that institutions should motivate communitarian behavior because the core values of the new nation were communitarian and success was represented by civic virtue and commitment to each other. The nation would prosper politically, economically, and socially, this group argued, to the degree to which civic virtue and commitment to each other were cherished and encouraged.

These two visions of successful civic behavior have competed with each other in one way or another over the course of the nation's history, as Marone (1990) has well demonstrated, but as the examination in this book has shown, over time the evolution of important institutions—citizenship, political economy, and the public sphere and government—have resulted in the scales tilting heavily in favor of the self-interest motivation. These institutions did not evolve in a vacuum, but here I have examined them separately to draw out the distinctive influences of each one separate from the others.

In the early years of the new nation, citizenship was limited to only those able to carry out the important obligations and duties that came with being a citizen, the most important of which in a democratic republic was to cast a vote. This very limited view of citizenship was rooted in classical thinking about the obligations that the virtuous had to society. When Aristotle says that a good citizen must know how to govern like a freeman and to obey like a freeman, he is characterizing a person of standing, whose actions will be for the good of the community because they can be for the good of the community. A freeman is free materially, intellectually, physically, and financially, and this freedom allows for independence of action. This was the way the founders saw the grant of citizenship.

However, this view of citizenship did not square with the idealistic language in the Declaration of Independence and the U.S. Constitution, which talked about political equality. And so, over time and as a result of a continuous struggle to make the practice conform to the ideals, citizenship was expanded. And as citizenship was expanded, the very meaning of citizenship changed: the institution of citizenship changed. By the time it was a universal grant, that is, by the time all Americans 18 years of age and older could vote, citizenship referred to rights and privileges rather than duties and obligations. The motivation for participation in the early years of the nation's history was to carry out a civic obligation; indeed, in those early years to be a citizen was to participate for the good of society. By the middle of the twentieth century, to be a citizen was to have rights: the right to vote and the right to other social, economic, and political benefits. Lost in the historical evolution of the institution of citizenship was the civic duty motivation.

During and in the years following the founding period, the American economy was largely an agrarian one with very small bits of manufacturing and industry in the bustling cities on the coast. The major ports at Boston, New York, Philadelphia, Baltimore, and Norfolk provided access to international trade. For many founders this political economy was exactly what the new nation needed because it would, they argued, incentivize a communitarian-oriented sense of civic duty that would produce civic virtue in Americans. It would, on one hand, encourage independence but, on the other hand, also encourage a concern for neighbor, community, and nation. Others argued that America should move rapidly toward a manufacturing economy based upon the initiative and labor of individuals attempting to succeed. Such an economy would make America strong internationally, and that strength, respected around the world, would lead to civic pride, and it would be this pride that would translate into a strong civic commitment to the nation.

The two approaches to political economy incentivized civic participation differently, one encouraging a communitarian-civic duty behavior and the other encouraging a self-interested behavior. Almost immediately, the agrarian-based communitarian approach began to lose ground to the manufacturing-based individual approach. And as the American political economy evolved over two centuries, both approaches gave way to a consumer-oriented self-interest approach that encouraged the notion that consumption was in fact an act of civic duty, and one of the only acts of civic duty that the consumer-oriented political economy valued.

One of the most persistent debates in contemporary American politics is about how large the public sphere should be and how active the national government should be within that public sphere. In fact, this debate has its roots in the American founding, and has carried on ever since. While there was certainly disagreement around the edges, the founders mostly agreed that the national government should be small and that most public problems should be handled by the states or in individual communities. The reason for this belief is rather simple. From a republican perspective, problem solving is best handled at the local level because it is at this level that individuals are most likely to subordinate their own interests to the interests of the whole. A small and inactive national government would not threaten the civic participation and sense of civic obligation that existed in communities. The further removed from the people a problem was solved, the more likely there was to be corruption and greed, and the less likely individuals were to be willing to subordinate their own interests to the interests of the whole. A larger public sphere and more active national government were not only more likely to be corrupt, but also less likely to incentivize civic participation or encourage a sense of civic duty. Thus, the size of the public sphere and the level of governmental activity were directly related to the extent to which people acted out of a sense of civic duty or self-interest. Over time, the public sphere widened and the national government became involved in solving problems—both big and small. This happened because people demanded that it happen. Some problems were seen as too big for local or state solutions. And as the national government became more involved in problem solving at every level of society, the civic duty incentive for participating in problem solving diminished.

The way in which these institutions have evolved has altered at the macro level the calculus of participation. If at the nation's founding the motivation for participation was primarily a civic duty one, by the middle of the twentieth century the overriding motivation for participation was a self-interested one, which meant participation happened when it was in the individual's self-interest to participate. The institution of citizenship, which originally encouraged participation out of a sense of civic duty, no longer did this by the late twentieth century. The nation's political economy, which originally incentivized economic behavior that resulted in communitarian-oriented concerns, encouraged self-interested consumerism by the middle of the twentieth century. The size and scope of the public sphere and the activity level of government, which was small at the nation's beginning, had become so all-encompassing by the late twentieth century that civic-minded community problem solving was difficult at best.

Civic participation ebbs and flows and changes character over time. A primary force for the evolution of civic participation in America, I argue, has been the evolving nature of the institutionally structured incentives, which have influenced the motivations for participation. However, amidst institutional evolution, the process of socialization should act as a force for stability—a ballast, if you will—inculcating in citizens the formal and informal norms, customs, routines, and conventions of a society. The institutional agents of socialization, primarily the family, school, and media, act as a stabilizer for society in normal times, and a countervailing force pushing back against forces that would disrupt society in difficult times. However, in the last half century, just as the institutional changes described in this book appeared to converge and dramatically alter the calculus for participation, these institutional agents of socialization were themselves experiencing changes that hindered their ability to act as either a stabilizing or countervailing force.

The family is the most important agent of socialization, and the positive socialization benefits transmitted by the family are largely dependent upon the presence of two-parents. Since 1960, the percentage of children growing up in single-parent homes has increased by nearly 200, a trend that has made it less likely that the family as an agent of socialization has been as effective at teaching the customs, norms, traditions, and behavioral expectations. Schooling is where people learn about the civic and political system and acquire loyalties to the country and to democratic practices. The school system has an important role to play in training children to participate in democracy and self-governance. Until the 1960s, this was done through purposeful education on the workings of government and the responsibilities of citizens. However, in the 1970s school curriculum began to change, focusing less on civic responsibility and the workings of government and the political system and more on topics related to political behavior and disagreement, comparative politics, and contemporary events. The media has traditionally provided information about civic and political issues and about the political process. However, in recent decades the media has focused far more on scandal and corruption and much less on the information citizens need to understand the sometimes complex civic and political issues facing society. Additionally, the media has largely become an adjunct of the consumer-oriented political economy, encouraging self-interested consumption at nearly every turn. As a result, the media has come to play a less constructive socializing role.

In sum, by the later part of the twentieth century, the macro-institutional incentive for civic participation was self-interest, and the institutional forces that would normally mediate those self-interest incentives with a sense of civic obligation were unable to do so. The net effect was lower levels of participation in nearly all ways in which it is measured.

WHY DOES THIS MATTER?

Peter Levine, the philosopher and civic education scholar, argues that broader civic participation is important and beneficial to society for several reasons. For one, active and engaged citizens, through private voluntary and nonprofit associations, compliment the work of a successful state by creating and maintaining a strong civil society. Broad political equality is more likely where there is broad civic participation, and much less likely where only narrow segments of the population participate. The political system listens closely to those who speak up and limitedly to those who do not. Broad civic participation also results generally in better functioning public institutions because the institutions benefit from the collective energy of the people. Additionally, everyone has needs that can only be addressed collectively, and so these needs are more likely to be known and addressable when participation levels are high. Broad civic participation also encourages a robust and independent cultural life. Finally, Levine argues that civic participation is intrinsically valuable; that is, it has "potential dignity that is absent in many other forms of life" (2007, ch. 2).

There can be little reason to argue with Levine here, but there is something else: underlying my focus on the influence of history and institutions on civic participation in America is a concern about the nature and quality of participation. An assumption of much of the scholarship on civic and political participation, especially that of the dominant behavioral approach is that more is better, simply. The goal is to understand why voting rates, for example, are lower than we might want or expect them to be so that we can find ways to raise them because the higher they are the better is our democracy. But the nature and quality of participation is as important if not more important than the level of participation. Yes, higher rates of civic participation would be good in the abstract, but higher rates for what reason and at what cost? If increasing voting rates by 10 percent, for example, has no measurable effect on our ability to solve common problems such as poverty, the quality of education, or health care, or any number of society's other big concerns, then what is it worth? And worse, what if these additional voters have little or no understanding of the issues about which they are voting? Indeed, the results may be harmful because the higher participation rates may suggest broad consensus around a solution where none really exists. At some point it simply becomes a numbers game, and a potentially unhealthy numbers game at that.

An important corrective to this is the underlying motivation for participation. As I suggested in the first chapter, the motivation for participation has implications for the health of American society, both political and nonpolitical. America needs its citizens to be motivated by a sense of civic duty because of the civic health side effects that sense of civic duty produces, either in the form of social capital or the recognition that the civic whole is greater than the sum of individual interests. People who are motivated by self-interest are less likely than those who are motivated by a sense of civic obligation to participate broadly in the life of their communities. Instead, self-interest is likely to motivate them to participate only when they have a personal narrow stake in the outcome: here one day and gone the next. As a result, they are probably also less likely to consider the broader ramification of their choices on society. This point is articulated precisely by Campbell in reference to voting in the conclusion of his study of the role of schools and communities in civic life:

> What we want is an electorate in which, because of voters' sense of civic obligation, turning out to vote is the default option. Rather than deciding to vote only when they see an overt threat to their interests, voters would make voting a habit. Knowing they were coming to the polls would then

lead them to weigh their options carefully, as there is no reason that dutiful voters cannot also be informed. (2006, 195)

Without a certain level of civic participation motivated by a sense of civic obligation, some problems will simply be too difficult if not impossible for society to solve. It seems clear from this perspective that the extent to which civic participation is motivated more by self-interest and less by civic duty is the extent to which American society is potentially worse off.

We want broad civic participation then, but we want people to participate in the civic life of their communities, state, and nation for the right reasons. If we have that, then we also have something else that is important to society: public responsibility. Renewing the idea of public responsibility was one of the pleas of Purdy in *For Common Things*. Public responsibility is, for Jedediah Purdy, the perpetuation of things that society must hold in common or risk losing altogether: "We take our stance toward public life in the way our work, relationships, and general way of living affect the commons. The commons are the things we all rely upon that can be preserved only by attention running beyond narrow self-interest" (1999, 185–186). Public responsibility, he notes, does not have the qualities of much of the last 100 years' worth of civic participation.

Understanding the influence of history and institutions on civic participation in America is important because it helps us better understand not only our attitudes toward civic participation, but also why civic participation has waned. It also helps us understand something about the quality of civic participation. The quality of civic participation is what is important here, and our institutions have a powerful influence on that quality.

LEARNING FROM HISTORY

If it is important to understand the role of history and institutions in our contemporary civic participation problem, then it is also worth understanding the lessons that history can teach us about how we might try to respond and what we might expect as we go forward. America has shown time and time again that it is a vibrant society of innovative people. Our political, social, cultural, and economic institutions both allow for and encourage innovation and the entrepreneurial spirit. As Schudson (1998), Putnam (2000), Levine (2007), and many others have observed, the reforms brought on by the Progressive Era (roughly the late nineteenth century to the early 1920s) continue to shape not only the ways in which we expect people to participate, but also the standards by which we evaluate their participation. Some of the most important civic organizations in America were created during this era, including the Salvation Army, the Urban League, the Lions Clubs, the Boy and Girl Scouts, the Brookings Institution, Goodwill Industries, the PTA, the NAACP, the YWCA, and the League of Women Voters, to name a few. But, just as the progressive reformers of the late eighteenth and early nineteenth centuries envisioned new and innovative ways in which citizens would participate in the civic and political life of their communities and country, so too must we in the early twenty-first century be able and willing to envision new and innovative ways for participation today and into the future.

The progressive movement was, as Marone describes it, a "sprawling movement" with reform efforts that spanned the social, economic, cultural, and political landscape of America (1990, 98). There was, to be sure, no centralized or uniform program upon which progressive reformers agreed. There were also no clear political lines upon which progressive reformers crossed or avoided. There were thousands of progressive-minded politicians at the state and local levels from across the political spectrum. All three major presidential candidates in 1912, for example, advocated progressive causes. Many of the reforms were enacted over a several decades period, and thus the Progressive Era was not dramatic or sudden, either. However, by the time the Tennessee legislature ratified the Nineteenth Amendment on August 18,

1920, few people in America had been untouched by the reforms of the Progressive Era. And, as Cooper notes, the agenda set during the first two decades of the twentieth century still dominate American life today (1990). Most notably for civic participation, out of the Progressive Era came the idea that citizens should engage broadly and directly in the civic and political life of their communities and nation.

The Progressive Era reforms were the results of social, economic, cultural, and political forces. While the late nineteenth century and early twentieth century was a period of great economic growth, this economic growth also exposed an unease that rippled through society. These ripples could be seen most clearly during the depression of the 1890s, when nearly 15,000 companies and 500 banks failed, and unemployment reached as high as 19 percent (Hoffman 1970). The resulting labor unrest at the Homestead and the Pullman strike were crushed by coordinated corporate and government power, and Coxey's "army" (and several other armies of workers) was turned away from Washington with brute and legal force.

These populist outbursts reflected the competing realities of the period: while economic growth generally benefited everyone over time, the disparity in wealth was very real and growing at any given point in time. As much as a quarter of the workforce was out of work for some period of time in the late nineteenth and early twentieth centuries (Painter 1987). Thus, in the midst of economic growth unmatched in the nation's history existed a broad economic uncertainty expressed most evidently in the labor movement's pursuit of equality and self-worth. This economic uncertainty led to general uncertainty, as McCormick noted: "Amid hard times, many Americans questioned the adequacy of their institutions and wondered whether democracy and economic equality were possible in an industrial society" (1990, 103–104).

If there was an undercurrent (at times stronger and at other times weaker) of economic uncertainty during this period, there was outright distrust of government. At no time up to that point in history had the public's view of government been so low. Part of that poor standing, Wiebe argues, had been the result of the extraordinary efforts at reconstructing the former states of the Confederacy, an effort that resulted in failure and left many people across the country with a sense of political betrayal (1967, 5). But more fundamentally, the disruption in governing and public policy-making that resulted from the Civil War carried into the next several decades. Fraud and corruption were so endemic during the two terms of Ulysses S. Grant that one contributor to the *Century Magazine* bemoaned the dishonesty in politics. "Fraudulent contracts, sinister legislation, bought and paid for by those whom it benefits, trading of offices and votes, and all the various methods of robbing the public for the benefit of a few, have become so common among us as hardly to awaken surprise when exposed to the public view. There is, moreover, a close connection between the dishonest practices of politics and those of commerce . . ." (White 1963, 365–366).

Corruption in government was, of course, related to corruption in the party politics of the time and transmitted through the spoils system. While party loyalties ran deep in the late nineteenth century, dissatisfaction with the two major parties was ever-present as reflected in the numerous third party movements of the time. Party attachments were strong because the two major parties called on the values their followers learned at home and in their churches, of their shared community histories, and of their ethnic and religious identities. Republicans reminded voters that theirs was the party of morality that had abolished slavery and preserved the Union. Democrats reminded voters that theirs was the party that defended states' rights and individual liberty against an overbearing national government (McCormick 1990, 96).

Yet, dissatisfaction with party politics as usual was strong enough to spawn active third party efforts. Disenchantment with the politics of the Grant administration led to a Liberal Republican effort to block his reelection. Another group of

Republicans formed the Prohibitionist Party and ran candidates for several elections, as did the National Party. Like these, other smaller third parties met a similar failure at the ballot box. The third party that had the most influence was the People's Party, or the Populists, but even they were not able to challenge the two major parties for long (Calhoun 1996). One reason the two major parties held such control was corruption, where party politics became a job involving bribes, jobs for supporters, levies on office holders' salaries, and payments for votes. While patronage was common in the national government, it was rife in the large cities across the country (Painter 1987).

Society itself was changing as well, and much of that change could be seen, felt, and heard in the increasingly crowded cities filled with people who looked different, spoke different languages, and came from across the globe. Cities became magnets for people looking for jobs and new lives, both made available by the industrial revolution. Between 1870 and 1920, cities across the country doubled, tripled, and quadrupled in size. Boston's population went from 250,526 in 1870 to 748,060 in 1920. Los Angeles' went from 5,728 to 576,673 in the same time (Still 1974, 210–211). Improvements in urban transportation and the increased need to provide city services led to the centralization of power and machine politics, and ultimately to a call for reform in municipal governance. Much of the corruption of city and state governments was uncovered by muckraking journalists such as Henry and Charles Adams, W.T. Stead, Upton Sinclair, Gustavus Myers, and of course Lincoln Steffens. For the most part, their objective was to understand their society and the changes it was going through (Hofstadter 1955).

How did America respond to all of this? The standards by which we think about, try to teach, and want to measure civic participation certainly have their roots in the American founding, but have their modern footing in the reforms that were a response to all of this. In their totality, the Progressive Era social, economic, and political reforms summed to a newly adjusted vision of American democracy. While gathering everything under such a big canopy can often mean that, in fact, there is little there besides broad classifications, there was a set of common elements beneath the sprawling umbrella of Progressive Era reforms. Taken together, those elements made possible new and innovative ways for civic participation.

First, out of the progressive movement came an embrace of science and new approaches to public policy problem solving. There was a great faith in modernity that both helped spawn the progressive movement and matured as a result of that movement. This could be seen no more clearly than in the growth and development of the social science disciplines, which brought to bear an analytic method focusing on data to understand the human condition. Even the meaning of the term "science" evolved. Science no longer referred to a grand design whose fundamental principles could be comprehended and applied, but now came to describe a method, a procedure, and an orientation rather than simply a body of results (Wiebe 1967, 147).

Across the country, social scientists formed national organizations, established themselves in land-grant universities, and went about the task of using the scientific method to carefully analyze the complexities of society. Faith in science to promote democratic social progress was a basic element of progressivism in America, if not in Europe (Frezza 2007). This is exemplified no better than by John Dewey, the philosopher and educational reformer who argued that social problems were essentially scientific problems that required trained experts to solve. This necessitated, then, the education of the public in the scientific method because the public had an important role to play in judging the knowledge developed by the experts. Science and the role of experts had, for Dewey and many other progressives, a very democratic feel to it. The scientific method, applied to social problems, would produce a body of knowledge from which the public could then choose its preferred solution (Dewey 1927, 139). And in order for the public to have the ability to make such choices, Dewey argued for changes in the educational system to reflect the social and interactive nature of education and learning. Schools should be a breeding ground for democracy, where people learned how to live to their fullest potential (Dewey 1915).

In addition, the method of reform was innovative in its civic participatory implications as well. McCormick describes progressive reformers tackling a problem in this way:

> They typically began by organizing a voluntary association, investigating a problem, gathering relevant facts and analyzing them according to the precepts of one of the newer social sciences. From such an analysis a proposed solution would emerge, be popularized through campaigns of education and moral suasion, and—as often as not, if it seemed to work—be taken over by some level of government as a public function. Behind this method of reform lay a confidence that social science offered the means for remedying the conflicts of an industrial society. If the facts were gathered and properly understood, reforms could be found that genuinely benefited everyone. The Progressive's approach also reflected their growing faith that government could be trusted to solve problems. Most reformers did not initially set out to enlarge the government; they placed their faith first in private organizations. Over time, however, they looked increasingly to public agencies to carry out their programs. (Foner 1990, 107–108)

Second, out of the progressive movement came a set of economic reforms that were rooted in an ideological shift related to the role of government in the economy. Prior to the Progressive Era, the dominant view of the role of government in the economy was that government had a limited role if any: laissez-faire determinism was the norm. However, laissez-faire determinism gave way to a willingness and desire to expand the scope of governmental authority over the economy. Despite their specific reform interests, Kennedy argues, a common commitment to the positive state united progressives generally (1971). After 1900, nearly all major public policy proposals involved broad government action, especially at the federal level (Higgs 1987).

While the federal government received the bulk of attention concerning economic reforms, all levels of government were involved. Indeed, most of the early reforms such as regulations of corporations and the enactment of health and safety regulations in factories were done at the local and state levels. But, to most progressives leaving reforms in the hands of local and state government was tantamount to not really reforming. As Foner notes, progressives saw the need for the national government to be involved in reforms to address problems that were national in scope: poverty, economic insecurity, and a lack of industrial democracy. They would create the social conditions for true democratic freedom (1998, 153).

Among some of those major reforms were the regulation of food and drug quality in 1906, mine safety in 1911, institution of a household income tax in 1913, the creation of an agency to administer antitrust laws and the establishment of a central bank in 1913, and enactment of an eight-hour work day in 1916. These sweeping actions of economic regulation represented an alternative to a laissez-faire environment that allowed narrow interests to manipulate politics and public policy, and progressives saw them as a means to better civic participation. As Croly argued, it was necessary to use Hamiltonian means to achieve Jeffersonian ends (1914).

Finally, out of the progressive movement came a set of political reforms that collectively enhanced democratic citizenship and broadened civic participation. Much of the reforms began at the local level. For instance, in an effort to clean up city politics from the graft and corruption exposed by Muckraking journalists like Lincoln Steffens in *The Shame of the Cities*, cities began to enact reforms such as the city manager form of government and the commission form of government, which made it more difficult for machine politics to take root and flourish. At the state level, reform-minded governors such as Theodore Roosevelt of New York, Robert M. LaFollette of Wisconsin, and Woodrow

Wilson of New Jersey encouraged such electoral reforms as the secret ballot, the recall election, the direct primary, and the initiative and referendum election. These reforms were designed to make government more responsive to the people and their needs.

In addition to the economic and regulatory reforms at the national level, some national electoral and participatory reforms also happened. The most important and far reaching was, of course, the passage of the Nineteenth Amendment in 1920 that granted suffrage to women. The Seventeenth Amendment provided for the direct election of the American senators, subjecting them to the will of the votes rather than varied interests at the state legislative level across the country. Finally, procedural and rule changes in the operations of the U.S. House of Representatives ensured more public access to the workings of that body.

Collectively these reforms constituted a fundamental revision of civic participation in America, largely by removing barriers to direct citizen participation and, where complete removal was not possible, exposing the process to citizen view and input. They represented both new and revised ways for citizens to participate in a society undergoing rapid and profound transformation.

INNOVATIVE CIVIC PARTICIPATION

I have spent a considerable amount of time looking backward, but will close by briefly looking forward. Taken together, the evidence and arguments presented in this book make the case that institutions matter when it comes to understanding civic participation in America. Institutional arrangements and institutional orientations have shaped the civic behavior of Americans from the founding of the country, and continue to do so to this day. They have done so and continue to do so by broadly encouraging and discouraging different types of behavior, and as a result of broad historical changes in several key institutions, the predominant incentive today seems to discourage civic participation for reasons of civic obligation and instead encourage civic participation for reasons of self-interest.

The goal of this study is not to offer a prescription, but rather to try to understand the role history and institutions have played in shaping civic participation up to this point in our history. However, let me offer some thoughts on the prescriptive side in closing. Progressive reformers were concerned about the health of American democracy, and were looking for new and creative ways for people to participate more and more directly in the civic and political affairs of their communities, states, and nation. While the specific circumstances are certainly different 100 years on, this is precisely what observers of civic participation in America today are concerned about. Progressive reformers were optimistic, and shared a belief that modernity and progress were going to be good for democracy. They shared a belief in the ability of people to improve their environment through continuous effort. Progressive reformers were also innovative, creative, and bold in their reform efforts. Guided by the scientific method, they would study a problem and try nearly any experiment to overcome it. Their ultimate goal was to plan and construct a better future rather than leaving it to chance that a better future would develop.

The founding documents anticipated an active and engaged (and entrepreneurial) citizenry. The U.S. Constitution, for example, stipulates that all powers not explicitly given to the states or to the federal government are reserved to the people. The idea that the citizenry would take a leading and important role in the civic affairs of their communities and nation is rooted in the founding political philosophy of our society. As has been noted in an earlier chapter, de Tocqueville observed the unique propensity of Americans to form associations to tackle problems. America has always been a civically innovative and entrepreneurial society, and it is this innovative and entrepreneurial spirit that we should look to as a response to the institutional and historical forces discouraging civic participation for reasons of civic obligation and instead encouraging civic participation for reasons of self-interest.

Indeed, it is the entrepreneurial and creative spirit that may very well be the key to responding to the situation in which we find our nation by allowing us to weave a path between self-interest and civic obligation. Entrepreneurship and entrepreneurial skills are typically thought of in relation to profit-seeking self-interested motivations and behaviors, but applied to broader civic problems, they have the potential to combine the best elements of entrepreneurial thinking within a broader civic setting. Borrowing from Bornstein and Davis (2010), civic entrepreneurship[1] involves citizens building or transforming institutions to advance solutions to social or civic problems. Civic entrepreneurship does not ask citizens to abandon self-interest, but rather to turn entrepreneurial skills that might often be directed at a self-interested activity or goal toward an activity or goal with a larger civic or social benefit. Among the first to write about this form of entrepreneurship was Dees (2001), who characterizes civic entrepreneurs as change agents who work toward creating public value (as opposed to private value), who pursue new opportunities to accomplish their goals, who continuously adapt and learn, who act boldly, and who hold themselves accountable for the outcomes of their efforts.

In an age where institutional forces push in the self-interested direction far more than they push in the civic obligation direction, civic entrepreneurship has the potential to strike just the right balance, especially with younger citizens. Why is this? Because it makes participation in civic affairs possible in new and innovative ways that not only have the potential to counter some of the aspects of traditional forms of civic participation that are distasteful or confusing to young people (too conflictual or the lengthy time to see progress, for example), but also to make available avenues for participation that are new and innovative.

The nature of civic participation involves four characteristics that, if viewed through the civic entrepreneurship lens, may make them more accessible to younger citizens. First, civic participation often involves conflict. This is the most distasteful and confusing aspect of civic participation, especially political participation, for most people. A vast body of scholarship demonstrates the extent to which citizens of all ages, but especially younger citizens are turned off by partisan conflict and thus avoid political activities and engagement as much as possible. Civic entrepreneurship makes it possible to engage civically in ways that are less conflict-oriented. While a certain level of partisan (or ideological) conflict is inevitable in a democratic society, civic entrepreneurship is more often project or object-oriented and thus very practical, which could also give some context to the inevitable conflicts and debates. As opposed to being asked to join a partisan cause that has little practical impact on their lives, or take a position in an ideological or normative debate, which is difficult at best to link to their own day-to-day existence—two things that young citizens are often encouraged to do, civic entrepreneurship encourages them to take an active role in addressing practical civic problems that they find themselves interested in or drawn to.

Second, civic participation is a public activity as opposed to a private activity. Civic entrepreneurship applies the skills and knowledge of a business enterprise, which is oriented toward the maximization of private profits, to the social and civic world where the goal is to address needs that are distinctly public in nature. This allows, in some small way, for people to turn their skills and orientations—normally being pushed in the self-interested direction—to civic needs.

Two other aspects of civic participation are less difficult to meld with civic entrepreneurship. Civic participation is seldom a solitary act, and neither is civic entrepreneurship. The term civic relates to a concern about community and people. Civic participation and civic entrepreneurship both involve collaboration to achieve some positive change for people and/or communities. Finally, both civic participation and civic entrepreneurship are voluntary at their core. However, while traditional forms of civic participation might always and forever be voluntary (such as voting, serving on the PTA, or contributing money to a cause), civic entrepreneurship activities might in fact allow the entrepreneur to earn a profit.

This last point is what makes civic entrepreneurship such an appealing potential answer to the institutional forces pushing in the direction of self-interested behavior and away from civic duty behavior. Civic entrepreneurship has the potential to bridge these institutional forces in a way that is positive and constructive, and in keeping with the broader sense of civic duty articulated by Jefferson and others. We know that for many reasons young people avoid or have limited exposure to political participation (for instance, see Zukin et al. 2006 and Colby et al. 2007 for two recent studies), but civic entrepreneurship offers a methodology for participation that could lead to a new kind of Progressive Era, where seemingly intractable social and economic problems get addressed in new, innovative, and creative ways and transform society in the process. As Sagawa (2006) characterizes it, the Progressive Era saw extensive entrepreneurship in the civic arena that spawned new institutions on an unprecedented level. These new institutions relied on volunteers and did not necessarily look to government to fund or spread their efforts, but ultimately had a significant impact on public policy over the course of the last 100 years.

I have described how the evolution of the macro-institutions of citizenship, political economy, and the public sphere and size of government have affected the motivation for participation by incentivizing self-interested participation over civic obligation, but I am not advocating retrenchment. While citizenship would be better served as an institution if citizens felt a greater sense of civic duty than they do, universal suffrage and the citizenship rights that come with it make America better without question. While the consumer-oriented market economy probably encourages more waste and needless want than is desirable, it has helped millions of Americans move into the middle class and we are better for it. And while the size and scope of the public sphere is in constant need of restraint, government activity has done far more to improve the quality of human existence than it has to harm it, especially in the last 75 years.

We are where we are. The past is the past, and vibrant societies seldom go backward. Our goal is to find new and creative ways for civic participation, and civic entrepreneurship might illuminate a path through the institutional forces by mixing a smidgen of Hamiltonianism with a dash of Jeffersonianism to find our way to a new kind of civic participation for the twenty-first century.

Notes

Chapter 1

1. Incidentally, of those who said they did not vote, which were not many, the number one reason given was a lack of time and the number two reason given was failure to register to vote on time.
2. See *The Letters of Thomas Jefferson*, Electronic Text Center, The University of Virginia Library at http://etext.virginia.edu.
3. The Center for the Constitution at James Madison's Montpelier survey can be found at http://center.montpelier.org/survey/highlights.
4. The Civic and Political Health of the Nation report can be found at http://www.pewtrusts.org/our_work_report_detail.aspx?id=19762. The Rockefeller Foundation report on National Service and Civic Engagement can be found at http://www.rockfound.org/initiatives/amer_workers/121807us_service.ppt.
5. I use the term "Church" to refer to all religious institutions.
6. In actuality the rate is likely a percentage point or two higher because the National Baptist Convention, U.S.A., Inc. did not report membership data to the Yearbook in 1998, 1999, and 2000.

Chapter 2

1. "The States Ratify Full Vote at 18," *New York Times*, July 1, 1971, p. A1.

Chapter 3

1. See the transcripts of this exchange at: http://www.cnn.com/SPECIALS/cold.war/episodes/14/documents/debate/
2. http://www.whitehouse.gov/news/.

3. http://www.fordham.edu/halsall/mod/1942roosevelt-sacrifice. html.

Chapter 4

1. http://www.cpsc.gov/businfo/cpsa.pdf.

Chapter 5

1. See the full report at http://nass.org/index.php?option=com_ content&taxk=view&id=132&itemid=45
2. Derrick DePledge and Sergio Bustos, "Poll: Young People See Voting as a Choice, Not a Duty," *Decision 2002: Gannet News Service Special Report* (October 31, 2002).
3. See the full report at http://center.montpelier.org/survey/ highlights.

Chapter 6

1. While many writers use the term "social" rather than "civic," I use the term "civic" because of its broader application to both the social and political.

References

Abramson, Paul R. 1983. *Political Attitudes in America*. San Francisco: W. H. Freeman.

Adams, Henry, and Earl N. Harbert. 1986a. *History of the United States of America During the Administrations of Thomas Jefferson*. Library of America. New York: Literary Classics of the United States.

———. 1986b. *History of the United States of America During the Administrations of James Madison*. Library of America. New York: Literary Classics of the United States.

Allen, Frederick Lewis. 1952. *The Big Change*. New York: Harper & Row.

Allen, W. B. 1988. *George Washington, A Collection*. Indianapolis, IN: Liberty Fund.

Almond, Gabriel A., and James S. Coleman, eds. 1960. *The Politics of the Developing Areas*. Princeton: Princeton University Press

Almond, Gabriel A., and Sidney Verba. 1963. *The Civic Culture*. Princeton: Princeton University Press.

Arendt, Hannah. 1963. *On Revolution*. New York: Viking.

Atkins, Charles K., and Walter Gantz. 1978. "Television News and Political Socialization." *Public Opinion Quarterly* 42: 183–198.

Bandura, Albert. 1977. *Social Learning Theory*. Englewood Cliffs, NJ: Prentice-Hall.

———. 1986. *Social Foundations of Thought and Action*. Englewood Cliffs, NJ: Prentice-Hall.

Banning, Lance. 1978. *The Jeffersonian Persuasion*. Ithaca: Cornell University Press.

Barbalet, J. M. 1988. *Citizenship*. Minneapolis: University of Minnesota Press.

Barnes, Albert H. 1964. *The Anti-Slavery Impulse*. New York: Harcourt, Brace & World.

Bellah, Robert N., Richard Madsen, William M. Sullivan, Ann Swidler, and Steven M. Tipton. 1991. *The Good Society*. New York: Vintage Books.

Benedict, Michael Les. 1991 "The Constitution of the Lincoln Presidency and the Republican Era." In *The Constitution and the American Presidency*, eds. Martin Fausold and Alan Shank. New York: SUNY Press.

Bennett, Stephen E. 1997. "Why Young Americans Hate Politics, and What We Should Do About It." *PS: Political Science and Politics* 30: 47–52.

Berlin, Ira. 1974. *Slaves Without Masters*. New York: Pantheon Books.

Berkowitz, Edward D. 1991. *America's Welfare State*. Baltimore: Johns Hopkins University Press.

Berman, Morris. 2000. *The Twilight of American Culture*. New York: W. W. Norton & Co.

Bornstein, David, and Susan Davis. 2010. *Social Entrepreneurship*. Oxford: Oxford University Press.

Buhl, Mari Jo, and Paul Buhl. 2005. *Woman Suffrage*. Urbana, IL: University of Illinois Press.

Butts, R. Freeman. 1978. Public Education in the United States. New York: Holt, Rinehart, and Winston.

———. 1980. *The Revival of Civic Learning*. Bloomington, IN: Phi Delta Kappa Educational Foundation.

Burns, Rex. 1976. *Success in America*. Amherst, MA: University of Massachusetts Press.

Cain, William E., ed. 1995. *William Lloyd Garrison and the Fight Against Slavery*. Boston: Bedford Books.

Calhoun, Carles W. 1996. *The Gilded Age*. Wilmington, DE: Scholarly Resources.

Campbell, Angus, Gerald Gurin, and Warren E. Miller. 1954. *The Voter Decides*. Evanston, IL: Row, Peterson, and Company.

Campbell, Angus, Philip E. Converse, Warren E. Miller, and Donald E. Stokes. 1960. *The American Voters*. New York: John Wiley & Sons.

Campbell, Ballard C. 1995. The *Growth of American Government*. Bloomington, IN: Indiana University Press.

Campbell, David E. 2006. *Why We Vote*. Princeton, NJ: Princeton University Press.

Catterall, Ralph C. H. 1903. *The Second Bank of the United States*. Chicago: University of Chicago Press.

Chaffee, Steven H., Scott Ward, and Leonard Tipton. 1970. "Mass Communication and Political Socialization." *Journalism Quarterly* 47: 647–659.

Chute, Marchette. 1960. The *First Liberty*. New York: E. P. Dutton.

Civic Participation Activities Guide. n.d. Austin, TX: Holt, Rinehart and Winston.

Clark, Nadine I., James B. Edmonson, and Arthur Dondineau. 1954. *Civics for Americans*. New York: The Macmillan Company.

Cohen, Lizabeth. 2003. *A Consumers' Republic*. New York: Alfred A. Knopf.

Colby, Anne, Elizabeth Beaumont, Thomas Ehrlich, and Josh Corngold. 2007. *Educating for Democrcys*. San Francisco, CA: Jossey-Bass.

Coleman, James S. 1988. "Social Capital in the Creation of Human Capital." *American Journal of Sociology* 94: S95–S120.

Cooper, John Milton, Jr. 1990. *Pivotal Decades*. New York: W. W. Norton.

Coxe, Tench. 1794. "A View of the United States of America." Philadelphia: William Hall and Wrigley & Berriman.

Croly, Herbert D. 1914. *The Promise of American Life*. New York: Macmillan.

Cultrice, Wendell W. 1992. *Youth's Battle for the Ballot*. Westport, CT: Greenwood Press.

Dalton, Russell J. 2008. *The Good Citizen: How A Younger Generation is Reshaping American Politics*. Washington, D.C.: CQ Press.

Davis, Kenneth S. 1986. FDR *The Dew Deal Years 1933–1937*. New York: Random House.

Dawson, Richard E., Kenneth Prewitt, and Karen S. Dawson. 1977. *Political Socialization*, 2nd ed. Boston: Little, Brown and Company.

Dees, J. Gregory. 2001. *The Meaning of "Social Entrepreneurship."* http://caseatduke.org/dowcuments/dees.sedof.pdf.

Delli Carpini, Michael X., and Scott Keeter. 1996. *What Americans Know about Politics and Why It Matters*. New Haven: Yale University Press.

Dennis, Jack. 1968. "Major Problems of Political Socialization Research." *Midwest Journal of Political Science* 12: 85–114.

Democratic Party, and Oliver A., Jr, Quayle. 1936. *Official report of the proceedings of the Democratic national convention held at Philadelphia, Pennsylvania, June 23rd to June 27th, inclusive, 1936, resulting in the re-nomination of Franklin D. Roosevelt <of New York> for president and John N. Garner <of Texas> for vice-president*.

Dewey, John. 1915. *The School and Society*. Chicago: University of Chicago Press.

———. [1916] 1966. *Democracy and Education*. New York: Free Press.

———. 1927. *The Public and Its Problems*. New York: Henry Holt.

Djupe, Paul A., and J. Tobin Grant. 2001. "Religious Institutions and Political Participation in America." *Journal for the Scientific Study of Religion* 40: 303–314.

Easton, David. 1965a. *A Framework for Political Analysis*. Englewood Cliffs, NJ: Prentice-Hall.

———. 1965b. *A Systems Analysis of Political Life*. New York: John Wiley & Sons.

Easton, David, and Jack Dennis. 1969. *Children in the Political System*. New York: McGraw-Hill.

Easton, David, and Robert D. Hess. 1962. "The Child's Political World." *Midwest Journal of Political Science* 6: 229–246.

Ellis, Richard E. 1987. *The Union at Risk*. New York and Oxford: Oxford University Press.

Elson, Ruth Miller. 1964. *Guardians of Tradition*. Lincoln, NE: University of Nebraska Press.

Fallows, James. 1996. *Breaking the News*. New York: Pantheon.

Farkas Steve, and Ann M. Duffett. 2010. *High Schools, Civics, and Citizenship*. Washington, D.C.: American Enterprise Institute.

Farrand, Max, ed. 1966. *Records of the Federal Convention of 1787*. New Haven: Yale University Press.

Fehrenbacher, Don E. 1987. *Lincoln in Text and Context*. Stanford, CA: Stanford University Press.

Foner, Philip S. 1983. *History of Black Americans*. Westport, CT: Greenwood Press.

Foner, Eric. 1990. "From Slavery to Citizenship," in *Voting and the Spirit of American Democracy*, ed. Donald W. Rogers. Urbana, IL: University of Illinois Press.

———. 1998. *The Story of American Freedom*. New York: W. W. Norton.

Ford, Paul Leicester, ed. 1904–1905. *The Works of Thomas Jefferson*. New York: G. P. Putnam's Sons.

Frank, Thomas. 1997. *The Conquest of Cool*. Chicago: University of Chicago Press.

Franklin, Benjamin. 1987. *Writings*. New York: The Library of America.

Franklin, John H. 1961. *Reconstruction*. Chicago: University of Chicago Press.

———. 1967. *From Slavery to Freedom*. New York: Vintage Books.

Frezza, Daria. 2007. *The Leader and the Crowd*. Athens, GA: University of Georgia Press.

Gallman, Robert E. 1960. "Commodity Output, 1839–1899." In *Trends in the American Economy in the Nineteenth Century*. Studies in Income and Wealth, Vol. 24. Princeton, NJ: Princeton University Press.

Garramone, Gina M., and Charles K. Atkins. 1986. "Mass Communication and Political Socialization." *Public Opinion Quarterly* 50: 76–86.

Gecas, Viktor. 1989. "The Social Psychology of Self-Efficacy." *Annual Review of Sociology* 15: 291–316.

Gillespie, James M., and Gordon W. Allport. 1955. *Youth's Outlook on the Future*. Doubleday papers in psychology, 15. Garden City, NY: Doubleday.

Gimpel, James G., J. Celeste Lay, and Jason E. Schuknecht. 2003. *Cultivating Democracy*. Washington, D.C.: Brookings Institution.

Greenberg, Edward S. 1970. *Political Socialization*. New York: Atherton Press.

Greenstein, Fred. 1965. *Children and Politics*. New Haven: Yale University Press.

Grofman, Bernard, Lisa Handley, and Richard G. Niemi. 1992. *Minority Representation and the Quest for Voting Equality*. Cambridge: Cambridge University Press.

Hall, Peter A., and Rosemary C. R. Taylor. 1996. "Political Science and the Three New Institutionalisms." *Political Studies* 44: 936–957.

Hess, Robert D., and Judith V. Torney. 1967. *The Development of Political Attitudes in Children*. Chicago: Aldine.

Hesseltine, William Best. 1963. *Lincoln's Plan of Reconstruction*. Confederate centennial studies, no. 13. Gloucester, MA: Peter Smith.

Higgs, Robert. 1987. *Crisis and Leviathan*. New York and Oxford: Oxford University Press.

Hill, Napoleon. 1937. *Think and Grow Rich*. Meriden, CT: Ralston Society.

Hixson, Walter L. 1997. *Parting the Curtain*. New York: St. Martin's Griffin.

Hoffman, Charles. 1970. *The Depression of the Nineties*. Westport, CT: Greenwood.

Hofstadter, Richard. 1955. *The Age of Reform*. New York: Alfred A. Knopf.

Hougland, James G., and James A. Christensen 1983. "Religion and Politics: The Relationship of Religious Participation to Political Efficacy and Involvement." *Sociology and Social Research* 67: 405–420.

Hughes, R. O. 1923. *Elementary Community Civics*. Boston: Allyn and Bacon.

Hyman, Herbert H. 1959. *Political Socialization: A Study in the Psychology of Political Behavior*. Glencoe, IL: Free Press.

Hyman, Herbert H., Charles R. Wright, and John Shelton Reed. 1975. *The Enduring Effects of Education*. Chicago: University of Chicago Press.

Ignatieff, Michael. 1995. "The Myth of Citizenship." *The Ideal of Citizenship Since Classical Times*, Ronald Beiner, ed. Albany: SUNY Press.

Inaugural Addresses of the Presidents of the United States. 1989. Washington, D.C.: U.S. Government Printing Office.

James, Scott. C. 2005. "The Evolution of the Presidency: Between the Promise and the Fear." In *The Executive Branch*, eds. Joel D. Aberbach and Mark A Peterson. Oxford: Oxford University Press.

Jefferson, Thomas (Eds. Andrew Adgate Lipscomb, Albert Ellery Bergh, and Richard Holland Johnston). 1904. *The Writings of Thomas Jefferson*. Washington, D.C.: Issued under the auspices of the Thomas Jefferson Memorial Association of the United States, 15: 450.

———. 1954. Notes *on the State of Virginia*, William Harwood Peden, ed. Chapel Hill: University of North Carolina Press.

Jennings, M. Kent, and Richard G. Niemi. 1974. *The Political Character of Adolescence*. Princeton: Princeton University Press.

Kaplan, Marshall, and Peggy L. Cuciti. 1986. *The Great Society and Its Legacy*. Durham, N.C.: Duke University Press.

Kapur, Jyotsna. 1999. "Out of Control: Television and the Transformation of Childhood in Late Capitalism," in *Kids' Media Culture*, ed. Marsha Kinder. Durham, NC: Duke University Press.

Kazin, Michael. 1995. *The Populist Persuasion*. New York: Basic Books.

Keller, Morton. 1990. *Regulating a New Economy*. Cambridge: Harvard University Press.

Kennedy, David M., ed. 1971. *Progressivism*. Boston: Little, Brown.

———. 1999. *Freedom From Fear*. New York and Oxford: Oxford University Press.

Kerber, Kindra K. 1995. "Ourselves and our Daughters Forever." In One *Woman, One Vote*, ed. Marjorie Spruill Wheeler. Troutdale, OR: NewSage Press.

Keyssar, Alexander. 2000. *The Right To Vote*. New York: Basic Books.

Kilgore, Harley M. 1943. "Old Enough to Vote." *The Spotlight* 1:6.

Kline, Stephen. 1993. *Out of the Garden*. London: Verso.

Kymlicka, Will, and Wayne Norman. 1994. "Return of the Citizen: A Survey of Recent Works on Citizenship Theory." *Ethics* 104: 352–381.

Ladd, C. Everett. 1996. "The Data Just Don't Show Erosion of America's 'Social Capital.'" *Public Perspective* 7: 1–6.

Ladd, C. Everett. 1999. *The Ladd Report*. New York: Free Press.

Lane, Robert E. 1959. *Political Life*. Glencoe, IL: Free Press.

Lasn, Kalle. 1999. *Culture Jam*. New York: HarperCollins.

Lasswell, Harold. 1950 [1932]. *Politics: Who Gets What, When, How*. New York: P. Smith.

Lawson, Steven F. 1976. *Black Ballots*. New York Columbia University Press.

Leach, William. 1993. *Land of Desire*. New York: Pantheon.

League of Women Voters of Cleveland. 1999. *The Youth Vote*. Cleveland: League of Women Voters of Cleveland Educational Fund.

Leuchtenburg, William E. 1963. *Franklin D. Roosevelt and the New Deal*. New York: Harper & Row.

Levine, Peter. 2007. *The Future of Democracy*. Medford, MA: Tufts University Press.

Litt, Edgar. 1963. "Civic Education, Community Norms, and Political Indoctrination." *American Sociological Review*, 28: 69–75.

Madison, James. 1999 [1787]. "No. 10: The Same Subject Continued." In *The Federalist Papers*, Clinton Rossiter, ed. New York: Mentor.

————. 1865. *Letters and Other Writings of James Madison, Published by order of Congress,* ed. Philip R. Fendall. 4 volumes. Philadelphia: Lippincott.

Magruder, Frank Abbott. 1948. *American Government.* Boston: Allyn and Bacon.

Malone, Dumas. 1970. *Jefferson the President: First Term, 1801–1805.* Boston: Little, Brown.

Mann, Mary. 1868. *Life and Works of Horace Mann.* Boston: Horace B. Fuller.

Marone, James A. 1990. *The Democratic Wish.* New York: Basic Books.

Marshall, Thomas H. 1950. *Citizenship and Social Class and Other Essays.* Cambridge: Cambridge University Press.

McCormick, Richard L. 1990. "Public Life in Industrial America, 1877–1917." In *The New American History,* ed. Eric Foner. Philadelphia: Temple University Press.

McCoy, Drew R. 1980. *The Elusive Republic.* Chapel Hill: University of North Carolina Press.

McKeon, Richard. 1941. *The Basic Works of Aristotle.* New York: Random House.

Merriam, Charles E. 1931. *The Making of Citizens.* Chicago: University of Chicago Press.

————. 1934. *Civic Education in the United States.* New York: Scribners.

Mutz, Diana C. 2006. *Hearing the Other Side.* New York: Cambridge University Press.

Nash, Gerald D., Noel H. Pugach, and Richard F. Tomasson. 1988. *Social Security The First Half-Century.* Albuquerque: University of New Mexico Press.

Neale, Thomas H. 1983. *The Eighteen Year Old Vote.* Washington: Congressional Research Service.

Nelson, John R. 1987. *Liberty and Property.* Baltimore: Johns Hopkins University Press.

NEGP Monthly. 2000. Vol. 2, no.22. National Education Goals Panel: Washington, D.C.

Nie, Norman H., Jane Junn, and Kenneth Stehlik-Barry. 1996. *Education and Democratic Citizenship in America.* Chicago: University of Chicago Press.

Niemi, Richard G., and Mary Hepburn. 1995. "The Rebirth of Political Socialization." *Perspectives on Political Science* 24: 7–16.

Niemi, Richard G., and Jane Junn. 1998. *Civic Education: What Makes Students Learn.* New Haven: Yale University Press.

North, Douglass C. 1966. *The Economic Growth of the United States, 1790–1860.* New York: Norton.

Novak, Willaim J. 2003. "The Legal Transformation of Citizenship in Nineteenth Century America." In *The Democratic Experience,* eds. Meg Jacobs, William J. Novak, and Julian E. Zelizer. Princeton: Princeton University Press.

Painter, Nell Irvin. 1987. *Standing at Armageddon.* New York: W. W. Norton.

Pangle, Lorraine Smith, and Thomas L. Pangle. 1993. *The Learning of Liberty.* Lawrence, KS: University Press of Kansas.

Parsons, Talcott. 1990. "Prolegomena to a Theory of Social Institutions." *American Sociological Review.* 55: 319–333.

Peirce, Neal R. 1968. *The People's President.* New York: Simon and Schuster.

Peterson, Merrill D. 1966. *Democracy, Liberty, and Property.* New York: The Bobbs-Merrill Co.

Pierson, Paul, and Theda Skocpol. 2002. "Historical Institutionalism in Contemporary Political Science." *Political Science, State of the Discipline.* New York: W. W. Norton and American Political Science Association.

Piven, Frances Fox, and Richard A. Cloward. 1988. *Why Americans Don't Vote.* New York: Pantheon Books.

———. 2000. *Why Americans Still Don't Vote.* Boston: Beacon Press.

Plutzer, Eric. 2002. "Becoming a Habitual Voter." *American Political Science Review* 96 (March): 41–56.

Pocock, J. G. A. 1995. "The Ideal of Citizenship Since Classical Times." In *The Ideal of Citizenship Since Classical Times,* ed. Ronald Beiner. Albany: SUNY Press.

Purdy, Jedediah. 1999. *For Common Things.* New York: Alfred A. Knopf.

Putnam, Robert D. 1995. "Bowling Alone: America's Declining Social Capital." *Journal of Democracy* 6: 65–78.

Putnam, Robert D. 2000. *Bowling Alone.* New York: Simon & Schuster.

Ratner, Sidney, James H. Soltow, and Richard Sylla. 1979. *The Evolution of the American Economy.* New York: Basic Books.

Remini, Robert V. 1967. *Andrew Jackson and the Bank War.* New York: Norton.

Riesenberg, Peter. 1992. Citizenship *in Western Tradition*. Chapel Hill: University of North Carolina Press.

Robertson, Ross M., and Gary M Walton. 1979. *History of the American Economy*. New York: Harcourt Brace Jovanovich.

Rogers, Daniel T. 1978. *The Work Ethic in Industrial America, 1850–1920*. Chicago: The University of Chicago Press.

Rosenstone, Steven J., and John M. Hansen. 1993. *Mobilization, Participation, and Democracy in America*. New York: Macmillan.

Sabato, Larry J. 1993. *Feeding Frenzy*. New York: Free Press.

Sagawa, Shirley. 2006. *Fulfilling the Promise*. Cambridge, MA: New Profit, Inc.

Sandel, Michael J. 1996. *Democracy's Discontent*. Cambridge, MA: Harvard University Press.

Sanders, Elizabeth. 1999. *Roots of Reform*. Chicago & London: University of Chicago Press.

Sanford, Stefanie. 2007. *Civic Life in the Information Age*. New York: Palgrave Macmillan.

Santoni, G. J. 1986. The *Employment Act of 1946: Some History Notes*. St. Louis, MO: Federal Reserve Bank of St. Louis.

Schattschneider, E. E. 1960. *The Semisovereign People*. New York: Holt, Rinehart and Winston.

Schlesinger, Arthur M. 1944. "Biography of a Nation of Joiners." *American Historical Review*, 50: 1–25.

———. 1945. *The Age of Jackson*. New York: Mentor.

———. 1959. *The Coming of the New Deal*. Boston: Houghton Mifflin.

Schudson, Michael. 1998. *The Good Citizen: A History of American Civic Life*. New York: Free Press.

Seiter, Ellen. 1993. *Sold Separately*. New Brunswick, NJ: Rutgers University Press.

Shlaes, Amity. 2007. *The Forgotten Man*. New York: HarperCollins.

Shklar, Judith N. 1991. *American Citizenship*. Cambridge: Harvard University Press.

Sims, Anastatia. 1995. "Armageddon in Tennessee." *In One Woman, One Vote*, ed. Marjorie Spruill Wheeler. Troutdale, OR: NewSage Press.

Skocpol, Theda. 2003. *Diminished Democracy: From Membership to Management in American Civic Life*. Norman OK: University of Oklahoma Press.

Smith, Roger M. 1997. *Civic Ideals*. New Haven: Yale University Press.

Stanton, Elizabeth Cady, Susan B. Anthony, Matilda Joslyn Gage, and Ida Husted Harper, eds. 1970. *History of Woman Suffrage*. New York: Source Book Press.

Stewart, James B. 1976. *Holy Warriors*. New York: Hill and Wang.

Still, Bayrd. 1974. *Urban America*. Boston: Little, Brown.

Stone, Richard D. 1991. The Interstate Commerce Commission and the Railroad Industry. New York: Praeger.

Studenski, Paul, and Herman E. Krooss. 1963. *Financial History of the United States*, 2nd ed. New York: McGraw-Hill.

Taylor, Robert, Mary-Jo Kline, and Gregg L. Lint, eds. 1977. Papers *of John Adams*. Cambridge: Belknap Press of Harvard University Press.

Tedin, Kent L. 1974. "The Influence of Parents on the Political Attitudes & Adolescents." *American Political Science Review* 68: 1579–1592.

Teixeira, Ruy A. 1992. *The Disappearing American Voter*. Washington, D.C.: Brookings Institution.

Tocqueville, Alexis de. 1956 [1832]. *Democracy in America*. Ed. Richard D. Heffner. New York: Mentor.

Verba, Sidney S., and Norman H. Nie. 1972. *Participation in America*. New York: Harper and Row.

Verba, Sidney S., Kay L. Schlozman, and Henry E. Brady. 1995. *Voice and Equality: Civic Volunteerism in American Politics*. Cambridge, MA: Harvard University Press.

Verba, Sidney S., Kay L. Schlozman, and Nancy Burns. 2005. "Family Ties" in *The Social Logic of Politics*, ed. Alan S. Zuckerman. Philadelphia: Temple University Press.

Walker, John F., and Harold G. Vatter. 1997. *The Rise of Big Government in the United States*. Armonk, NY: M.E. Sharpe.

Wattenberg, Martin P. 2007 (2008). *Is Voting for Young People?* New York: Pearson Longman.

———. 2002. *Where Have All the Voters Gone?* Cambridge: Harvard University Press.

Watts, Steven. 1987. *The Republic Reborn*. Baltimore: Johns Hopkins University Press.

———. 2005. The *People's Tycoon*. New York: A. A. Knopf.

White, Leonard D. 1963. *The Republican Era*. New York: Macmillan.

Wiebe, Robert H. 1967. *The Search for Order.* New York: Hill and Wang.

Wills, Gary. 2005. *Henry Adams and the Making of America.* New York: Houghton Mifflin.

Williams, Chilton. 1960. *American Suffrage.* Princeton: Princeton University Press.

Wolfinger, Raymond E., and Steven J. Rosenstone. 1980. *Who Votes?* New Haven: Yale University Press.

Wolfson, Steven C. 2005. *Civics for Today.* New York: AMSCO School Publishing.

Wood, Gordon S. 1969. *The Creation of the American Republic.* Chapel Hill: University of North Carolina Press.

Wooddy, Carroll H. 1934. *The Growth of the Federal Government, 1915–1932.* New York: McGraw-Hill.

Yabiku, Scott T., William G. Axinn, and Arland Thornton. 1999. "Family Integration and Children's Self-Esteem." *The American Journal of Sociology* 104: 1494–1524.

Zukin, Cliff. 2000. "Across the Generational Divide." Paper presented at the annual meeting of the American Association for Public Opinion Research, Portland, May 19–21, 2000.

Zukin, Cliff, Scott Keeter, Molly Andolina, Krista Jenkins, and Michael X. Delli Carpin. 2006. *A New Engagement?* New York: Oxford University Press.

INDEX